"Pull up a chair and let this master destructive stories we often rely on t by narratives of stress-inducing sca Holberg invites us to instead live out truer narratives of abundant friendship and restorative hope. As the philosopher Alasdair MacIntyre has written, if we want to rightly answer the question, What am I to do? we must first answer the question, Of what story or stories do I find myself a part? Holberg is a wise guide to the faithful, life-giving stories that Christians are called to inhabit."

Jeffrey Bilbro, associate professor of English at Grove City College and author of *Reading the Times*

"Not only is Jennifer Holberg a clear, compelling, and beautiful writer, but her words in *Nourishing Narratives* are also filled with truth and goodness. I can't remember the last time I read a book that made my heart sing along as this one did. *Nourishing Narratives* will open your eyes, grow your faith, and feed your soul."

Karen Swallow Prior, author of *The Evangelical Imagination: How Stories, Images & Metaphors Created a Culture in Crisis*

"Funny and approachable, erudite and smart, this book is not merely a celebration of literature—it is an invitation to learn how to read as if our faith lives depend on it. Jennifer Holberg shows us why we love stories and, more importantly, why we need them."

James K. A. Smith, editor in chief of *Image* journal and author of *You Are What You Love*

"Threading her own stories with rich reflection on biblical narratives and on the novels and poems she has taught and loved, Jennifer Holberg offers here a beautiful way of understanding what it means to live by stories. *Nourishing Narratives* is a rich celebration of cookbooks, dog walking, Dante, college life, embracing solitude, and living in communities bound together by shared stories that equip them to see one another through whatever life brings. Every page offers food for thought and thanksgiving."

Marilyn McEntyre, author of *Caring for Words in a Culture of Lies* and *When Poets Pray*

"Wise, observant, and compassionate, Jennifer Holberg's *Nourishing Narratives* is a beautiful book that celebrates the readerly life of stories, novels, and poetry. With warmth and honesty, Holberg brings the worlds of writers from George Eliot to Dante into the trials of daily life. She inspires us to hold on to a 'vision of a light-filled world, full of sometimes difficult things,' as she puts it so well. I shall cherish this book."

Michelle Kuo, author of *Reading with Patrick*

Nourishing Narratives

THE POWER *of* STORY *to* SHAPE OUR FAITH

JENNIFER L. HOLBERG

IVP
Academic

An imprint of InterVarsity Press
Downers Grove, Illinois

InterVarsity Press
P.O. Box 1400 | Downers Grove, IL 60515-1426
ivpress.com | email@ivpress.com

InterVarsity Press® is the publishing division of InterVarsity Christian Fellowship/USA®. For more information, visit intervarsity.org.

All Scripture quotations, unless otherwise indicated, are taken from The Holy Bible, New International Version®, NIV®. Copyright © 1973, 1978, 1984, 2011 by Biblica, Inc.™ Used by permission of Zondervan. All rights reserved worldwide. www.zondervan.com. The "NIV" and "New International Version" are trademarks registered in the United States Patent and Trademark Office by Biblica, Inc.™

The publisher cannot verify the accuracy or functionality of website URLs used in this book beyond the date of publication.

Cover design: David Fassett
Interior design: Jeanna Wiggins

Cover Images: © oxygen / Getty Images, © Olaf Simon / EyeEm / Getty Images, Rawpixel.com

ISBN 978-1-5140-0524-8 (print) | ISBN 978-1-5140-0525-5 (digital)

Printed in the United States of America ♾

Library of Congress Cataloging-in-Publication Data
A catalog record for this book is available from the Library of Congress.

30 29 28 27 26 25 24 23 | 12 11 10 9 8 7 6 5 4 3 2 1

FOR MY BELOVED DAD,

who made every story possible,

and who embodies the most important story of all:

the amazing love of God

Contents

1

Complicated Narratives and Important Failures

I STILL HAVE THE HANDMADE BIRTHDAY CARD my fifth grade teacher gave me—an enormous piece of folded yellow construction paper with a big orange bookworm (wearing a festive birthday hat, naturally) drawn on the front. Somehow that flimsy relic of forty years ago survived the many moves of my childhood and found a snug home at the bottom of the cedar box a great-uncle made me as a repository for my "treasures."

Perhaps it's no surprise I safeguarded it so carefully: after all, it's certainly an unusual year when one is celebrated for being bookish—celebrated, more importantly, by the fabulously named Anquanita Ash. I mean, if that doesn't sound like a name straight out of some wonderfully magical story, I'm not sure what does. And Mrs. Ash *was* magical—one of those teachers who becomes an indispensable feature of childhood lore. Goddess of the fifth grade, she strode effortlessly through the halls of Carriage Hills Elementary School, cooler than most anyone else we had ever known.

One of the most memorable aspects of her classroom was how she handled reading. To be sure, she read aloud to us each day after lunch, and we had instruction in reading and spelling and the rest. But the great privilege was to be allowed time in the "reading tub": an old claw-foot bathtub that sat in one corner of the room. Its sides were lined with a vibrant red faux-fur material whose only other natural habitat appeared to be the dashboards of certain very groovy cars. The tub itself was filled with seemingly endless pillows of all sizes and varieties. So when our work was done, we were encouraged to luxuriate with a book, there among the pillows: reading as pleasure and reward. It was an important lesson: to read, according to Mrs. Ash, was not a grim chore of mastering subjects and verbs, but a task to be sought and savored and enjoyed.

This was a lesson of which, even at eleven years old, I'd been an eager pupil for a long time. For one thing, I had a grandmother who was well-known for her devotion to books. Other people might have Proustian memories of the smell of their grandmothers' cookies; my Grandma Kline's house smelled exactly like a very lovely used-book shop. Most rooms in her house featured floor-to-ceiling bookcases, with volumes overflowing the shelves' bounds. In her basement, each room was filled with canning shelves so that the books could be placed two-deep on them. Many of her books were from the nineteenth or first half of the twentieth century, and on my family's visits, I would spend hours combing the shelves, discovering all manner of Victorian literature, tales of faraway missionaries and theological treatises, histories of places and events of which I had never heard, cookery books, and more: a whole library's worth of subjects. She had so many books that she kept at least one grocery sack by her front door with those she had either read or of which she had inadvertently bought doubles. Visitors to her house always spent time finding at least one volume to take with them: reading as hospitality.

As a beloved grandchild, I was not limited to choosing from this front-door stash but had the full run of her collection, though my mother always insisted that I ask my grandmother for any book I wanted to have. I was never refused: reading as love. Indeed, I learned from my Grandma Kline that books could serve as vital companions on the journey; her wise, and typically wry, advice to me: "Always have at least one book in your purse at all times."

But it wasn't just my grandmother and Anquanita Ash who taught me these practices of reading; so did a family life characterized by nightly, communal novel and Bible reading, church and Sunday school experiences replete with both tale and interpretation, and scads of Bible memorization. Indeed, I had a story-shaped childhood. It is, doubtless, little wonder that I became an English professor.

But no matter what one's childhood—even if one was not or is not really much of a reader—we are *all* profoundly story-shaped people. We live in a world that, for better or worse, most often seems to process through narrative, not facts.

Think about it: from the time we are children, we use stories to imagine the possibilities life may offer us. Consider the stories you have told yourself over the years about what you would like to be or hope to do, what job you would have, where you might travel, what your wedding would look like, how many children or grandchildren you would have. Right now, I'd wager, you could tell me a story about what you think this next year will bring. We know the reverse is true as well: we can probably all think of examples of people whose lives get stuck because they can't imagine a different narrative for their lives, can't imagine living out a different story line. Think how many times you've heard someone say, particularly after a disappointment or a sudden tragedy or in the middle of a midlife crisis, "That's not what was supposed to happen."

Without dismissing the shock and sadness of these situations, I suggest it is telling that such a comment implies the existence of a story we all narrate to ourselves constantly—and how strongly it shapes our own responses. I still think about an example from many years ago: how Elizabeth Edwards, wife of the disgraced presidential candidate John Edwards, framed her answer when she was recovering from her husband's infidelity. In an interview she explained: "It's an ongoing process of finding your feet again, retelling your story to yourself. You thought you were living in one novel, and it turns out you were living in another."[1]

And it's not just the stories we tell—it's the ones we listen to, it's the ones we value, it's the ones we engage with and spend time interpreting. Through stories we come to understand the expectations and norms of others around us—our family, community, church, and larger culture. Indeed, stories define those expectations and norms—and signal to us whether our lives are successful or not (at least according to those doing the telling). That's no surprise—from at least the British Romantic poets, like Percy Shelley, we've been explicitly told that poets, storytellers, and people who control the imagination are the "unacknowledged legislators of the world."[2] Such a claim wouldn't have surprised Socrates, who saw the power of poets and, unlike Shelley, warned of their pernicious influence way back in the fifth century BCE. And of course, thinking through narrative is Jesus' primary pedagogical mode: a man goes on a journey, a woman searches for a coin, a son goes astray, a servant makes a bad investment. Whatever the perspective, there is ample evidence that societal attitudes—on whatever issue, whether toward smoking or politics, war or sexuality—are affected more by story than by law. Thus, stories both encourage and constrain us, depending on our ability to critically interpret and respond to these narratives.

This book, then, is not just for bookworms like me: it is for everyone hoping to think more deeply about what it means to be fundamentally story-shaped people, people hungry for narratives that are life-giving. Many wonderful books exist already to persuade you of the merits of reading certain books (often the "classics," for example) or journeying with certain writers. All good. But though the coming pages will invite you into a conversation with the work of many writers, this is not a book so much meant to prescribe *what* or *who* to read, but more about *how* and *why*. I am not going to claim that reading makes you somehow "better," but rather that becoming a better reader—more attuned to narrative assumptions and strategies and expectations—is critical.

And for people of faith, for people of the Book, this book considers how the larger story to which we give allegiance, the gospel— the overarching story of God's good creation; humanity's fall; and our redemption through the life, death, and resurrection of Jesus Christ—interacts with the smaller stories in which we participate. Not only because, as critic Henry Zylstra has argued, the discernment of stories should generally give us "more to be Christian with"[3] but because the old, old story must be fundamental to our very understanding of the world.

I once attended a conversation between the poet Christian Wiman and the theologian J. Todd Billings, both living with incurable cancers. At one point, the moderator asked why they were both interested in poetry. Billings responded by noting that he had turned to the Psalms because they were Scripture first, rather than because they were poetry. But then he framed what he called the "more interesting question": "Why did *God* choose poetry with the Psalms, with Job, with other parts of divine self-revelation in Scripture?"[4] Yes, why *is* God a literary God? In *Beyond Words*, Frederick Buechner begins to suggest at least one answer:

It is absolutely crucial, therefore, to keep in constant touch with what is going on in your own life's story and to pay close attention to what is going on in the stories of others' lives. If God is present anywhere, it is in those stories that God is present. If God is not present in those stories, then they are scarcely worth telling.[5]

Surely, then, it's good work for us to carefully examine the multi-faceted stories of all of our lives and learn to notice the infinite richness of the story of the Word made flesh.

BY NAME

Our stories begin with a name—our own—each with a tiny etymo-logical tale built in. I've always loved hearing the roots of names, whether in the Scriptures or in cultural practices. How cool is it, for example, that the day of the week on which a Ghanaian is born is reflected in their name? Or that the name Deborah in the Bible means "bee" (oh, the metaphorical possibilities!)? The meaning of my own name, Jennifer, confounded me a little bit as a child. I mean, I could easily see (and hear) the connection to the first meaning, the earlier name of "Guinevere," (even if she wasn't the most admirable person in the Arthurian story). But what of the second meaning from Cornish, "white wave"? What could it pos-sibly mean to be named after ocean surf? But the ancient Cornish folk found a crashing breaker winsome in its comely command. What I came to love is how my name preserves in miniature a story from a culture who loved and thrived off the sea, who saw that beauty and power could be present together—and wanted to capture it in the hopes they had for their daughters.

And names are a big reason why I love graduation day. Of course, I like volunteering at the senior picnic and seeing my students with their delighted families. I like meeting the parents and siblings, cousins and aunts and grandparents. I like putting on my gaudy "Husky Purple" robe (go, University of Washington!) and my funky Ye Olde English Hogwarts tam, even if, as I often joke, I most resemble the grape from the Fruit of the Loom gang in my getup. I like assembling with my peers, all snazzily dressed up as well, and marching in to the strains of "Pomp and Circumstance," even if I do feel bad every year for the band, forced to repeat the song eighty-seven times.

At Calvin University, we're still of a size that we call out the names of each graduate. It takes a while to get through them all, but my colleagues who read do so with such care and attention, reaching out to students to request phonetic renderings so they get each name just right. They know how critical that is—how much identity resides in every name.

Most years I know a good number of students—and as I hear their names and see them walk across the fieldhouse floor to accept our president's congratulations, I see them again as they were in my classes. It's not all sunshine and puppies, of course; though I often warmly remember their talent or intellect or personality, sometimes I am also bemused that they made it through to graduation at all.

But as I hear the litany of names, I hear not just a reminder of the stories of those I know. Clearly, in a class of a thousand or so people, many students are strangers to me. No, it is the very names themselves that move me. I am fascinated by how each name carries with it histories and genealogies and the chronicles of many generations. I imagine how each name was a name that parents wondered about and deliberated over, practiced saying fondly to each other aloud, perhaps intended with it something that honored folks who had come before them. That great Adamic privilege of naming, of imbuing another being with a hope and a future. Each name, to paraphrase Walt Whitman, then, "contains multitudes"—

the community of family and friends and church and teachers and
so many others who surround that student as he or she journeys
onward. The recognition of that, the understanding of the way we
are part of a much bigger story than ourselves, is moving, indeed.

I thought of the graduation ritual the other day when I was at
church. I typically sit farther toward the back, but because I was
one of the readers in the service, I had to sit in the front row. When
it came time for Communion, which we took by intinction—
coming forward to dip the bread into the cup—I realized I could
hear the pastors administering the elements. What particularly got
my attention was that as each person approached to receive the
bread, the minister would say his or her name:

"Sally, the body of Christ broken for you."

"Hiroyuki, the body of Christ broken for you."

"Yaa, the body of Christ broken for you."

And on and on through the many people in our large congregation. In the course of that Communion service, I heard the
names of the entire church—and heard again and again, too, about
Christ's death for each of them. I was surprisingly affected by what
seemed to me to be a wonderfully holy moment, a reminder that
even if our parents took no care with our names, we are still absolutely beloved of the God who calls us by name (Is 43:1) and died
for each of us by name too. There's a reason for all those genealogies in Scripture: God's story is no tale of abstraction, but a richly
detailed one. The story begins, then, with our own absolute particularity. In fact, part of God's work as "author and finisher" is not
simply knowing our names, but inscribing each of them, too, into
God's own book (Heb 12:2 NKJV).

The significance of inscription makes me think of Diet Eman, a
member of the Dutch Resistance whose work in World War II included rescuing Jews, gathering intelligence, and surviving stints

in concentration camps and as a fugitive herself. It was my privilege to host her many times in my first-year writing class. On her visits, she would bring items from her time in prison: a metal cup, some of her identity papers, and a piece of rope.

I think of that rope often.

Diet made the rope in a concentration camp, where one of the prisoners' jobs was to take long shreds of paper and weave them into braided cords. But this one was a little different: on the strips of paper, Diet wrote down the names and addresses of all the women in prison with her, before she wove the strands together. She swore to them that, when she was released, she would unravel the rope and go to each address to give their families an update. Until she was released, however, she wore the rope as a belt, telling the guards (in her typical, cheeky way) that she needed something to hold up her underwear.

Diet never undid the rope.

She didn't have to because she enacted the words of Proverbs 3:3, "Let love and faithfulness never leave you; bind them around your neck, write them on the tablet of your heart." She had memorized every name and every address. After her release, she visited every family, as she had promised, to deliver her news. And every time she came to my classroom, Diet brought herself and every one of those women who had suffered with her, bound in that fragile cord. What a powerful image of grace and remembrance—and how comforting to think about our names and the names of all who we love and every other name ever emblazoned on the vast tablet of God's own heart.

WHAT LANGUAGE SHALL I BORROW?

That all sounds wonderfully capacious, but life often doesn't feel like that. Instead, it feels like we are presented with a limited number of available narratives—or at least narratives we can allow ourselves. Have you ever felt trapped in a story presented to you by family or church or community?

Before we lament the impoverished messages of our larger culture, we need to have a good look at Christian cultural narratives. Many of my students, for example, are particularly fond of the classic "virtue is rewarded," believing that Jane Austen's Mr. Darcy is just around the corner if they can behave "properly." Ring by spring, anyone? What happens, though, at age twenty-five or thirty-five or (even!) forty-five, when Darcy has seemingly gotten lost in Derbyshire? The narrative gets a little wobbly. *Was one not virtuous? Or is God not giving what one is owed?* As it turns out, that particular story can't provide the "happily ever after" it promises.

More than that, the church has a tendency to send the message that some people's stories are more important than others. Or if not more important, perhaps, at least much more interesting, and surely much more valid in showing God's work in the world. Think about how the Christian genre of "testimony" has traditionally been presented.

The first time I was asked to give my testimony when I was in high school, I found the whole process of putting it together rather trying because I didn't seem to have much of a story. I became a Christian as a very young child, grew up in a strong Christian family that was at church whenever the doors where open (and sometimes, given my parents' volunteering, even when they weren't), and was a hyper-responsible, academically achieving student. No big traumas, no big catastrophes, no "big sins." Seemingly nothing more to narrate than "Woo-hoo—I'm a nerdy good girl."

I even teased my mother that perhaps I should go out before I had to speak and "spice things up a bit." I was suffering—as perhaps some of you are—from Boring Testimony Syndrome. Sure, my story was fine and all. No one would have said otherwise, but I secretly believed it couldn't compete with the *really* good testimonies. From years of going to church, I sensed that what was valued were two dominant narrative paradigms: the "super Christian" or the "miserable sinner."

The "super Christian" for me growing up was Elisabeth Elliot. When I was six years old, I saw the movie *Through Gates of Splendor*, based on her book about her husband and his fellow missionaries who died in the Amazon in the 1950s. Elliot's story was not just one of missionary martyrdom, but one in which Elliot returns to live with many of the same people who had killed her husband. In my 1970s and 1980s childhood and young adulthood, she was presented as the epitome of Christian discipline—never shrinking, always dutiful, fiercely all in. And it wasn't just Elliot: in the Christian comics we were given in Sunday school, we had stories about missionaries who smuggled Bibles behind the Iron Curtain and the like. Child of the Cold War that I was, I was so inspired that in late elementary school, my best friend, Jo Lynn Carter, and I would spend endless hours planning what we would do on the mission field, how we would customize our cars to be able to smuggle the maximum numbers of Bibles or help the most destitute people groups. Together, these stories set my expectations about what a successful Christian life needed to look like: heroic, epic, dangerous. Certainly never anything ordinary.

On the other side, the "miserable sinner" model was even more popular. The guest speaker invited to church to tell of a life of crime and drugs and all manner of depravity until he or she was converted. The dark-to-light quotient was very high indeed here with the "miserable sinner" now doing amazing, often heartwarming things.

These days, the dominant narratives may look a little different, but examine them and you'll see these roots showing. Admittedly, there is great validity present in both narratives. But we need to also admit that the majority of Christians' lives will never conform to those patterns. My students tell me they struggle with this. They're still suffering from the Boring Testimony Syndrome I experienced in my own adolescence: they think because they don't have an "exciting" life or some "big" sin to confess or a dramatic work of God in their life—a miracle or some triumph over adversity—that they don't have stories worth telling.

The consequences go beyond simply a dearth of available narratives: one significant result is that we develop a skewed sense of virtue and an equally skewed sense of sin. We subtly come to believe that there are people for whom faith is easy (at least easier than it is for us). We come to believe that faith needs to look a certain way and happen in certain contexts. We come to believe that there are people with "real" sins that need forgiving, but that our sins are minor in comparison and not worth talking about.

All of it wrong.

We also begin to believe, erroneously, that our stories have to have a demonstrably, conventionally dramatic plot line—because otherwise, we fear, there is no proof that God is working dramatically (or perhaps at all) in our lives.

The result of these faulty narrative expectations is we deny that God needs to transform our lives at every moment. Ironically, by tending mostly to these two extremes of the Christian story, we reduce God's power to accomplishing only the "big stuff." Instead, we urgently need to hear the stories of people who, no matter their background, are living a faithful life every day. Because the challenge of being kind and patient and forbearing and loving and generous and everything else we are called to do—loving the Lord our

God with heart, soul, strength, and mind and neighbor as ourselves (Mk 12:30-31) is very, very difficult—and only accomplished by the minute workings of God's grace.

But living into *that* story (and giving up on the dominant narratives as the only possibilities) may mean that we need to revise the story we thought we were living in or perhaps thought we needed to live in, even if it looks boring from the outside. It should help us revise, too, our narrative expectations so that we can begin to look for a fuller imagining. And that starts right where we are. In her beautiful meditation on Psalm 8, Marilynne Robinson puts it like this: "So I have spent my life watching, not to see beyond the world, merely to see, great mystery, what is plainly before my eyes. I think the concept of transcendence is based on a misreading of creation. With all respect to heaven, the scene of miracle is here, among us."[6]

What if we began to imagine our ordinary lives as "scenes of miracle"? How would that transform our sense of ourselves, our sense of God at work?

"COMPLICATED" NARRATIVES

Changing our narrative pattern to embrace "scenes of miracle" doesn't mean, though, that our stories should be chirpily naive or triumphalistically positive. Can we find better examples? In talking with many of my church-raised students, I've often heard them complain about how they heard the same handful of Bible stories again and again in their childhoods. Mostly, the "nice" stories—or if not exactly "nice" in reality, presented to them defanged of any problematic content. Typically, we conclude these discussions with much wise nodding and sage remarking on our preference for "complicated narratives." All very true, but I've found that our theoretical love for the "complicated narrative" is never quite as vigorous when we're actually faced with one. In real life, they're hard to tell, hard to interpret, hard to hear.

And seldom is that truer, especially for the literature professor in me, than when I'm the storyteller once a month to a large group of Sunday school kids who range from kindergarten to fifth grade. That's already a challengingly wide age range with whom to communicate. But recently, my church changed its curriculum to cover the whole Bible in-depth over a three-year period. Initially (see attitude above), I was pretty pleased: finally, something grittier and more honest. No cotton-ball lambs allowed here.

Until I started to get all the hard stories. Seriously—I was assigned Job. The whole book. Take that, Dr. Complicated Narrative.

I also got the story from Numbers where Moses sends the twelve spies into Canaan to assess it before the Israelites are supposed to go in. Except that when ten of the spies come back and tell about the fortified cities and the giants (along with the amazingly massive grapes), the people get freaked out and don't want to go in despite Moses' urging from God, and so most of that generation of people have to die by wandering in the desert for forty more years. Good times.

Now, I'm always down with a spy story (and who doesn't love giant grapes?), but what do you do with the rest of it with a group of elementary school-aged kids in front of you?

I don't think the answer is as important initially as the hermeneutical method—in other words, how do we learn to be better interpreters? I've begun to ask myself,

- Why does this story seem hard to me?
- What makes it hard? What makes me uncomfortable?
- What does that discomfort reveal about my actual theology (instead of my professed one)?
- Does my theology need an adjustment? Or is this a tension I need to embrace more fully?

- What is at the essence of this story? More specifically, what is the takeaway for me today? Is this something I can share with the kids? If not, what of the essence is age appropriate?

- How can I use this story to help kids feel open to asking their own questions, to normalizing that interrogating the text is what we *should* be doing as Christians?

My moral obligation to teach these stories well means I have to come to at least provisional terms with them myself (or discover why I can't): not just asking why the Israelites were afraid in this situation, but why am I afraid? What are the giants and fortifications that face me and that face the children I'm teaching? Surely, we understand that fear, that hesitancy, even as we ourselves are told of God's providence. What parts of ourselves need to die in the purifying wilderness before we can move more fully into God's promises? Are there ways that our attitudes (particularly perhaps our generational ones) are holding others back? Am I keeping folks in the desert because I'm too afraid to move forward in faith?

And what of our interpretation of our lives? Whatever the story line we're currently in, I wonder how we can be more generous readers every day. What would it take to not automatically assign motives to the characters who inhabit the story with us? What would it take to be empathetic, not so quick to always identify villains? What would it take to not flatten our lives' plot lines into easy goods and bads? What would it change if we were protagonist, not hero or heroine?

Maybe the truth of the matter is that we need to admit that they're all hard stories.

THE BLESSINGS AND THE CURSES

And then what?

I admitted at this chapter's opening to my childhood status as a bookworm. One of my fondest childhood memories is the weekly bringing home of an enormous stack of books from the library and heaping it next to the yellow easy chair in my bedroom. The progress of my reading was easily charted as the mound of books was shifted from one side of the chair to the other—only to be carted back to the library and returned for a whole new stack. What I don't remember is my parents ever restricting what I wanted to check out, though they were incredibly committed Christians. I read widely, never afraid that God was too small to go with me into whatever bookish land I traveled. But that hasn't always been the way Christians have responded to the issue of censorship. Each September brings Banned Books Week, an event established over thirty years ago because books—in schools, libraries, and bookstores—were being increasingly contested, and the organizers wanted to call attention to issues of censorship. Unfortunately, we know that these challenges are often from people of faith. If we are people of the Book, we have not always been the people of the books.

In her marvelous 1957 essay "The Church and the Fiction Writer," Flannery O'Connor begins by identifying the way the "average Catholic reader" approaches texts, dividing them into rigid, but inadequate, categories of "nature and grace." Inadequate because, as O'Connor argues, neither gives a full enough picture: "He has reduced his conception of the supernatural to pious cliché and has become able to recognize nature in literature in only two forms, the sentimental and the obscene."[7] In particular, O'Connor's provocative notion here that sentimentality and pornography are equally distorted readings is an important and challenging (maybe even surprising) claim, especially in the large parts of Christian culture that often only sees the "obscene" as objectionable. Instead, O'Connor argues that both are equally unfit representations because they are not grounded in the world in all its complexity. Both are reductive. Christians, then, should be as worried about the sentimental (and the bad theology that undergirds it) as they are about the more obvious problems of the obscene. This means that accepting the assumptions of the romantic comedy on the Hallmark Channel can be as damaging to our ideas about love and romance as the diminishment and dehumanization apparent in X-rated fare. It means recognizing and rejecting the "pious cliché" at work in so much of what Christians consume.

According to O'Connor, we can only gain a truer picture of reality by being committed to learning how to read in a more nuanced way. In her words, "Catholic readers are constantly being offended and scandalized by novels they don't have the fundamental equipment to read in the first place."[8] If we can acquire that "fundamental equipment," however, we can recognize the transcendent in unexpected places, in works that might surprise us because, O'Connor notes, they are often "permeated with a Christian spirit."

And with this orientation, in turn, comes what I find most encouraging about O'Connor's essay: her conviction that this robust engagement with fiction—with stories that offer "an honest fictional representation of life"—is a measure of strong faith, not evidence of a weak one, as is so often asserted.

> It is when the individual's faith is weak, not when it is strong, that he will be afraid of an honest fictional representation of life, and when there is a tendency to compartmentalize the spiritual and make it resident in a certain type of life only, the sense of the supernatural is apt gradually to be lost. Fiction, made according to its own laws, is an antidote to such a tendency, for it renews our knowledge that we live in the mystery from which we draw our abstractions.[9]

And this is not just O'Connor's idea. In Joshua 8:34-35, we get this paradigm of reading:

> Afterward, Joshua read all the words of the law—the blessings and the curses—just as it is written in the Book of the Law. There was not a word of all that Moses had commanded that Joshua did not read to the whole assembly of Israel, including the women and children, and the foreigners who lived among them.

Thus, the Scripture itself invites us to read *all* the words. The blessings and the curses alike. Without both, the story is incomplete.

THRILLED BY LOVE

I once heard a speech by Katherine Paterson, the extraordinary children's writer, in which she argued that "the consolation of the imagination is not imaginary consolation."[10] I've thought about that phrase a good deal, especially as the violence—both rhetorical and actual—of the twenty-first century seems to be only worsening. After Newtown and Orlando and Virginia Tech and Columbine and Charleston and Atlanta and Uvalde and and and—that brutal never-ending list—I have found myself both voluble and oddly inarticulate. There is so much to say—and yet so little. How can nothing change? I find that my own words feel insufficient. Paterson's assertion makes a radical claim: that our Christian hope is a deeply creative act where, in our gathering together, we continually narrate the promises of a God who loves us and is making all things new. Of course, we only see part of the story—and then dimly, and the challenge is that we must imagine the "what is to be" in the midst of the horrific "what is." But nevertheless, the invitation to live into a different story—to imagine something so diametrically opposed to most of the lessons that everything around us seems to be aiming to teach us—is not a call to false hope. Indeed, it is the only way to any sense of peace.

Paterson's words remind me of another work by a writer of profound hope: Dante, who has helped me imaginatively engage theological issues better than any other writer. Set as it is on Good Friday through Easter, the medieval *Divine Comedy* very consciously uses that timeline to highlight the saving work that the character Dante has lost sight of—and which loss necessitates the long trip through hell and purgatory to paradise itself. But as *Inferno*'s opening line reminds us, the epic that follows is not of only one man, it is "our journey."[11]

Though most readers perhaps best remember the journey's beginnings in *Inferno* when Dante and his guide, the poet Virgil, traverse hell and encounter the vivid stories of the sinners they meet there, another aspect that has always struck me is the richly imagined setting. It's not as if Dante and Virgil meet sinners while walking around a conventional fiery lake or something—no, instead, Dante creates a complete physical world that displays the full effects of the fall. Sin blights not just lives, but landscapes.

But blight can never be the whole story for the Christian. In Canto XII, Dante and Virgil climb in treacherous mountain terrain. As they descend, Dante wonders about the landscape through which they are passing, causing Virgil to realize that it has changed since his last journey that way. Before, the path had been clear, but now an avalanche has blocked the path and (as we find out later) destroyed some bridges. Naturally, this wasn't just any random earthquake: it was the great cataclysmic earthquake that accompanied Christ's death and descent into hell to rescue the pre-Christian elect.

In this small moment in the canto is a massive truth: in the avalanche, in the destroyed bridges is the resounding testimony that Christ's Easter-work changes even the landscape, even the infrastructure of hell itself. Here, the very rocks cry out to tell of God's redemptive work. And why? The best line in the canto: "I thought the universe felt love."[12] Or as another translation puts it: "I thought the universe was thrilled with love."[13] Christ's tender sacrifice changes everything, everywhere. Even in the depths of hell— nothing can stand against it. Here again is "blessing and cursing," here the consolation of imagination, indeed.

Dante's sublime literary adventures are a keen example of how literature brings us new ways to engage the oldest, most fundamental truths. But it's not enough to simply re-see: the pattern and proportion of the stories we consume the most often is also vital.

When I take students to Italy, we spend the good part of a morning at one of my favorite places in Florence: San Marco, home of the fifteenth-century painter Fra Angelico. In the (almost) decade Fra Angelico lived and labored there, he painted a number of well-known works, including a famous Annunciation painting that greets you as you ascend the stairs to the monks' living quarters. Much as I love the art in the public spaces of the monastery, something else really moves me. In each tiny cell, Fra Angelico painted an incredible fresco as a devotional aid for the brother who occupied that room. Imagine that: masterworks produced not for a noble patron but for the average believer. The commitment to encouraging the contemplation of the beautiful as central to cultivating a daily life of devotion.

When we go to San Marco, I instruct my class to enter each cell, examine its painting, and ask themselves, How does it help them more fully "see" the aspect of the life of Jesus that is represented? How might it have encouraged discipleship and right action in the man who lived with it? And how would this "seeing" every day have changed him over time?

My own favorite is an unusual painting of Martha. It's unusual because it's not the expected story of Martha in the kitchen, worrying over unneedful things. Instead, in the top third, Jesus prays

Figure 1.1. *Agony in the Garden* by Fra Angelico, Santa Croce Monastery, Florence

and converses with an angel. In the middle third, James, Peter, and John sleep. But in the bottom third, Martha and Mary are portrayed in their house, wide awake, reading and praying. It is women who are active, men who are passive. It is Martha who mirrors Jesus in prayer, and it is Mary who is engaged with the Word through reading. Imagine the mind of the monk who meditated on *that* story every day. And then, consider your central narratives. Because what we choose to paint on the metaphorical walls of our brains and hearts will surely shape the disciples we become.

AN IMPORTANT FAILURE

This chapter has attempted to lay out some beginning claims for why story is so central for the faithful Christian. The following chapters will continue to explore story's shaping power in specific aspects of our lives. At heart, the best engagement with literature, I believe, has to involve not just intellectual understanding and aesthetic appreciation, but a cultivation of certain habits of heart and mind. Fundamentally, those habits are a way to combat T. S. Eliot's diagnosis in the *Four Quartets* that we are people "distracted from distraction by distraction."[14] In an age dominated by social media, that's a convicting description. But Eliot's verdict is nothing new. In his *Institutes*, John Calvin puts it this way:

> And since the glory of [God's] power and wisdom shine more brightly above, heaven is often called his palace. Yet . . . wherever you cast your eyes, there is no spot in the universe wherein you cannot discern at least some sparks of his glory. You cannot in one glance survey this most vast and beautiful system of the universe, in its wide expanse, without being completely overwhelmed by the boundless force of its brightness.[15]

And yet, Calvin concludes, "Certainly however much the glory of God shines forth, scarcely one man in a hundred is a true spectator of it."[16]

Geneva in the 1500s, London in the 1940s, Grand Rapids in 2023: our condition is the same. Very few are attending to the "sparks of glory."

But it's not enough to simply pay attention—that could take all kinds of forms, many of which could be potentially destructive. No, we need to pay attention for a purpose, a purpose I foreground for my literature classes by beginning each semester considering a painting by Pieter Bruegel the Elder.

As the image is projected on the screen at the front of the room, I ask the students what stands out to them. Usually, it's in the painting's foreground: a man in a bright-red shirt and his horse are plowing a field. Or in the middle section, a man is tending sheep. Along the shore, a man crouches as ships are sailing along. In the background are mountains and a city. All in all, a bustle of human activity, everyone absorbed in the brightly colored business of living.

With so much going on, it's easy to miss the most important detail. Looking very carefully in the bottom right-hand corner—between the crouching man on land and the largest of the sailing ships at sea—you can see a pair of legs is upended out of the sea. In fact, at first glance, it's a tad unclear what the legs even are.

Until the painting's title, *Landscape with the Fall of Icarus*, gets added to the class's analysis. You probably remember the story of Icarus: he and his father, Daedalus, escape from their imprisonment by making wings out of feathers and wax. Although Icarus is warned to not fly too close to the sun, lest it melt his wings, he becomes so excited by the feeling of flying that he rises higher and higher until, of course, his wings melt, he falls, and he is drowned in the sea.

In Bruegel's representation, Icarus's fall has clearly happened just moments before, which makes it all the more remarkable that this dramatic and tragic story makes no impact on the witnesses in the painting. None of them seem to notice that it has happened. Or

Figure 1.2. *Landscape with the Fall of Icarus*, attributed to Pieter Bruegel the Elder, Royal Museums of Fine Arts of Belgium

worse, if they do notice, they don't act on what they see. Only seconds before, a person came falling out of the sky, yelling and flailing. He hits the water with a sound, too. And yet, with all that commotion not a head is turned.

The poet W. H. Auden noticed this odd response and wrote a poem about it (there's a long tradition in English of poems that comment on other forms of art, called ekphrastic poetry). In his ekphrastic poem "Musée des Beaux Arts," Auden reflects on the lack of reaction in the painting's people, observing

In Breughel's Icarus, for instance: how everything turns away

Quite leisurely from the disaster; the ploughman may

Have heard the splash, the forsaken cry,

But for him it was not an important failure; the sun shone

As it had to on the white legs disappearing into the green

Water; and the expensive delicate ship that must have seen

Something amazing, a boy falling out of the sky,

Had somewhere to get to and sailed calmly on.[17]

In a way, this painting—especially when refracted through the lens of Auden's poem—reminds me a little bit of the story of the good Samaritan, where the first two men that pass by the wounded man are not moved by the "important failure" that they see. Their busyness blinds them, and they don't act as their faith would have them act.

We can relate: we are all busy, we all have "somewhere to get to," but as a result, boys drown all around us, metaphorically, every day. Our lack of attentiveness has consequences.

I open my classes with the combination of Bruegel's painting and Auden's poem because I want to highlight for my students the thesis of the course: not only does literature show us the great need of the world and remind us of our responsibility to pay attention, but it also calls us to respond to the world's needs and to live out our part in God's story of redemption. My hope for my students—and for all of us people of the Book—is that we are never people who merely witness "something amazing" and then "[sail] calmly on" in the face of calamity.

Instead, literature must help us look to the margins to see the overlooked and the perishing. And not just to see but to turn our face unhesitatingly toward the "disaster" and embrace it as our very own "important failure," worthy not just of our attention, but of our most valiant efforts to rectify it.

We read to save the drowning boy.

Let's get started.

2

Enough

Earth's crammed with heaven,
and every common bush afire with God:
But only he who sees, takes off his shoes.

ELIZABETH BARRETT BROWNING,
AURORA LEIGH

ONE OF THE BEST PARTS of moving to my new condo was
that I finally got to build a custom bookcase for my cookbook collection. Indeed, on my realtor-guided first visit to the condo, that
empty nook in the kitchen immediately cried out for shelves and
for my hundreds of books to fill them. I knew I was home.

I've collected cookbooks since I was a child when I bought my
very first one, *How to Make Possum's Honey Bread, Skunk's Chocolate Sprinkle Bread, and Raccoon's Raisin Bread, Too*, at a Scholastic
Book Fair. I still prize all those early volumes, and though I do love
to cook, my cookbook collecting has always been about much more
than learning how to produce food: for me, reading cookbooks is
about uncovering rich sociologies and acquiring deep insight into
the real material conditions of people's lives. I'm particularly drawn
to older examples—little gendered histories, giving the reader a
peek into the social expectations of the time. In fact, each book is
as much a creative presentation of a world as any novel: entering

that world, one witnesses the norms of hospitality, the assumed skills (now often long vanished), and the available resources and ingredients (also oftentimes absent) that people had in a particular time and community.

Or sometimes what they were lacking—I have a cookbook that was published in England in 1947, titled *Wishful Cooking*, which is an entire cookbook of recipes that could only be made with prewar ingredients, then unavailable because of postwar rationing. The book's publication was about imagination, not practicality. To read it is to understand both the privations of the British postwar period as well as its prewar indulgences, and to be reminded again of the evocative place that food has always held in human memory.

My sister is also a cookbook collector (as were our mother and our grandmother), so when I visited her one summer, she showed me a cookbook she had recently acquired. Stuffed within the pages were loose recipes that the previous owner had scribbled down and stuck there for safekeeping. One of these completely grabbed my attention, and I immediately got my phone to take a picture. Here's what it recorded:

Johnny Cake
1 flour to 2 cornmeal
½ cup sugar
1 heaping tbsp. lard
¼ salt
3 cup Klaber milk (1/2 tsp. soda to ordinary sour milk,
      less or more soda if less or more sour milk)

Make a sloppy thick batter like this
Bake in a quick oven on grate like biscuits
This makes enough

Now, Johnny Cake has a long and venerable history in American cooking, dating all the way back to indigenous peoples, so in some ways this is a quintessential recipe. And there are so many things to love about this particular iteration: the old-school measurement of giving flour to corn meal in proportion, not cups; the inclusion of lard; the description of Klaber milk (and the funny reminder of how to vary the proportion of soda to sour milk); the instruction to make a "sloppy thick batter" (what would that look like exactly?); the lack of a temperature guide beyond "a quick oven." It tells you a great deal about the writer's acumen in the kitchen and the basic ingredients with which she was working (including finding an economical use for sour milk).

But the reason I took a picture of this recipe—what seized my imagination—was the serving size: "This makes enough," it claims.

Not serves 4–6.

Not makes one 9-inch pan.

Nope, "enough." A formulation of perfect contentment.

If we're honest, how rare it is to think that anything in our lives is, in fact, enough? Sometimes it's that there's too much—too much to do, too many demands on our time and energy. Or maybe we fear we ourselves are too much—too many feelings, too needy, too loud. Or, I suspect, that more frequently we worry about not having or being enough—not enough time, not enough talent, not enough resources. We have internalized stories about ourselves that highlight our failures or deficiencies. Insufficiency is the operational hermeneutic of our lives in so many ways.

This interpretative mode has been around for as long as there have been stories. At a conference, I gained a key insight into our propensity toward this kind of reading when I listened to theologian Walter Brueggemann powerfully parse this phenomenon in the lives of the ancient Israelites.[1] As slaves in Egypt, he observed, the Israelites lived in a culture that had a "fear of scarcity," which led to hoarding and concentration of wealth and to the oppression and enslavement of the poor. But it's not just the Israelites: for anyone living with such a scarcity mindset, Brueggemann argued, their daily narrative will focus on what they don't have, on the constant possibility of loss. In this mindset, people cling tightly to what is theirs—what if it is insufficient, or worse, what if someone is at the ready to snatch it away? Thus, even people who *do* have enough are still anxious, convinced that they do not. And importantly, when they feel that they don't have enough, they also are unable to share out of their (actual) abundance. No community is possible, then, because people remain profoundly insecure and self-protective of "their" stuff.

So strong is this narrative, Brueggemann argues, that when the Israelites leave Egypt and are in the desert, they still find this story tempting. Even though they have witnessed God's mighty rescue and are being led by God's visible presence, the story they tell themselves becomes one of lack, one in which God is failing them. This story is so powerful that they become desperate enough to consider returning to slavery, and with it to the seemingly safer, more comforting story where they can at least tell themselves that they are in control of what little they have. They believe the lie that they can care for themselves. The wonder of the manna and the quail, then, is not only a fulfillment of a very tangible daily need, but more importantly it introduces the "narrative of abundance"—that God *will* provide. Enough for every day. Without hoarding or anxiety, fear or—significantly and especially—even their own effort.

Even as we struggle with our fears of insufficiency, the attraction to the myth of self-sufficiency is particularly hard to shake. In his memoir *The Sacred Journey*, Frederick Buechner gives this poignant snapshot of the consequences of living into that story:

To do for yourself the best that you have it in you to do—to grit your teeth and clench your fists in order to survive the world at its harshest and worst—is, by that very act, to be unable to let something be done for you and in you that is more wonderful still. The trouble with steeling yourself against the harshness of reality is that the same steel that secures your life against being destroyed secures your life against being opened up and transformed by the holy power that life itself comes from. You can survive on your own. You can grow strong on your own. You can even prevail on your own. But you cannot become human on your own. Surely that is why, in Jesus' sad joke, the rich man has as hard a time getting into Paradise as that camel through the needle's eye because with his credit card in his pocket, the rich man is so effective at getting for himself everything he needs that he does not see that what he needs more than anything else in the world can be had only as a gift. He does not see that the one thing a clenched fist cannot do is accept, even from God himself, a helping hand.[2]

How, then, do we shift our mindset away from "going back to Egypt" and being self-sufficient, and instead, find narrative models that are grounded in the conviction of God's plenitude? Not with a prosperity gospel based in our performance, but with a story rooted in our total belovedness and our complete inability to save ourselves. Put another way: What would happen if the stories we tell about God and about ourselves proceed from our absolute conviction of his loving generosity *and* our own "enoughness"?

SIGNIFICANT LEFTOVERS

Of course, such stories are everywhere in Scripture. Indeed, one could argue that God's abundance is the central feature of the narrative arc of the Bible: from a garden full of good things to eat to John's portrayal of the final, glorious banquet of the Lamb. And in-between, the table and overflowing cup of Psalm 23; the widow's profusion of oil in 2 Kings 4 (a chapter that also includes a separate story about multiplied bread); the vision of Isaiah 25 where "the Lord of hosts will provide for all peoples a feast of rich food and choice wines, juicy, rich food and pure, choice wines" (Is 25:6 NABRE). Or we could view Jesus' earthly ministry as beginning with miraculously producing wine at the wedding of Cana and ending with the new wine of redemption produced by the shedding of his own blood. But it is clear that joyful celebration, feasting, and God's plenty are essential to God's grand story for humanity. And in places such as 1 Corinthians 11, there is a rejection of any partiality at that grand table.

And it is all based in what Makoto Fujimura has termed God's "gratuitous love."[3] As wondrous as the manna and quail story is, the true radicalness of that story finds its ultimate embodiment in Jesus' life. One of the greatest of the Gospels' abundance stories, Christ's feeding of more than five thousand people from the meager provisions of only two loaves and five fish, can be read as a reimagining and amplification of the daily meal provided to the Israelites in Exodus. Here, too, these five thousand plus folks are out in the wilderness with no means of getting food, and they are miraculously fed. But what if the most important part of that story is that there are leftovers? After all, it is one thing for a savior to feed us, but it is quite another for one to provide nourishment and then some. He feeds *them*—with leftovers. And then, as if such demonstration of abundance isn't enough, Jesus does it all again, feeding four thousand men as well as the women and children with them (Mk 8:1-9). Again, with leftovers. The repetition emphasizes that God's spectacular provision isn't ever a one-time deal. Nor do we have to wonder if there will be enough for our hunger. Christ is not a one-size-fits-all meal provider: whatever we need is there for us and way more besides. There can be no worries about taking more than our share or having enough to go around or hoarding because in the bread and the wine of his own sacrifice, Jesus provides us with more love and grace and mercy and joy than we can ever ask for or imagine. And then some.

But I think it would be a mistake to see abundance only in such large and lavish displays or in the grand vistas of imposing mountaintop and vast ocean that form the visual backdrop of so many praise music church slides. Part of cultivating a better eye for abundance is to begin to see it in all sorts of places. In her poem "Mindful," Mary Oliver begins by observing:

Every day
　　I see or I hear
　　　　Something
　　　　　　that more or less
kills me
　　with delight,
　　　　that leaves me
　　　　　　like a needle
in the haystack
　　of light.
　　　　It is what I was born for—
　　　　　　to look, to listen,
to lose myself
　　inside this soft world—

> to instruct myself
>
> over and over
>
> in joy
>
> and acclamation.[4]

What if Oliver's mode was our goal for each day: to find something that "kills us with delight"?

Some years ago, my department invited our college president to join us for a lunchtime visit. Before he came, we met together to discuss how we'd like to use the hour we had with him. Of course, like academics everywhere, we had many "concerns" we wanted to make sure he heard. But we also decided that we wanted him to know about the good stuff too—the many things that gave us joy. And so that's how the meeting began: with a colleague reading a compilation of what we loved about our daily work. I thought it was an especially important exercise. It's just so much easier to default to critique—and that's certainly necessary and important. But I've been wondering more and more of late about how we cultivate joy in the midst of the mess. As my guide, I take words from Calvin's sermon on 1 Corinthians: "There is no tiny blade of grass, no color in the world that is not made to make men's hearts rejoice."[5] How can we better listen to this plenteous testimony: the idea that the creation is to engender rejoicing? In her own inimitable way, Mary Oliver echoes Calvin in her conclusion to "Mindful."

> Nor am I talking
>
> about the exceptional,
>
> the fearful, the dreadful,
>
> the very extravagant—
>
> but of the ordinary,

the common, the very drab,

the daily presentations.

Oh good scholar,

I say to myself,

How can you help

but grow wise

with such teachings

as these—

the untrimmable light

of the world,

the ocean's shine,

the prayers that are made

out of grass?[6]

Much as I love Calvin's and Oliver's formulations of wonder, it's certainly not always easy to follow them. Full confession: I am not "craft-y." I do not own a hot-glue gun. (NB: This is no judgment on ownership of said hot-glue gun, which seems like a handy thing to own, to be honest.) And I'm quite impressed by people who know how to quilt and crochet, paint and sew and the like. In any case, I somehow decided that making a gag gift would be "fun" and found myself in a craft store. From the reaction of the women who I met there (staff and customers alike), it was clear I looked lost or at least in desperate need of some help. Of course, they were not wrong in that perception. I imagine I looked slightly stunned. Who could have predicted the cavernous magnitude of a store that in no way resembled any lobby that I have ever seen? As I wandered through the store, looking for the one thing I had come for (and for which I was told there were three possible locations, seemingly miles apart),

I had not realized that the fake-botany industry extended to every conceivable species and color—not just flowers in all the hues of the rainbow but pumpkins and more squashes than I've ever seen at any farmers' market. I was amazed at the rows upon rows of mysterious objects for the creation of all manner of handiwork. And I struggled to fathom that so many surfaces existed for the presentation of glitter or, in fact, that an entire aisle of glitter choices was even a possibility. Who knew of glitter's rich diversity?

Was some of the store tacky and/or kitschy? To be sure. But I realized it was also rather wonderful. Here was a place that presented tangible evidence of the God-given desire to create beauty (even if that did mean glitter and artificial vegetables). And what if it did? Are not the knitting of a sweater, the compilation of a photo album, and the decorating of a home holy and beautiful acts? A small part of the restoration of the world? A bringing of order and shalom? A celebration of God's presence with us, even in the very ordinary? To the Creator of the universe, I'm not sure that the aesthetic differences between "art" and "craft" are perceived in as widely divergent terms as we may see them. To be honest, to God it probably all most closely resembles the macaroni projects of preschool. But God does not seem to love us any less for trying to participate fully and imaginatively in God's world.

I think Gerard Manley Hopkins might have enjoyed the craft store too. In my view, Hopkins is in the running for best Christian poet ever. His poems are dense and delightful, faithful and fraught, innovative and idiosyncratic yet insightful. They bear reading again and again, each time yielding something beautiful and brilliant. During his own short life—he died of typhoid at age forty-four—Hopkins celebrated the glorious design of God's world and each creature's distinctive place within it (he called this distinctiveness "inscape," short for inner landscape). When that inner landscape is projected out into the world through action (he called this "instress"), the result testifies to God's individual stamp on each thing in creation. By extension, then, Hopkins's poetry, which chronicles this process, helps the reader see anew this wondrous work. Even in his later "Terrible Sonnets," where he struggles intensely with depression and spiritual sterility, Hopkins continues to look for even the smallest moments of grace to peek through.

In his poem "Pied Beauty," he celebrates the wonder of creation, even in seemingly unconventional, unlovely, and unexpected things and places. And he also writes in praise of "áll trádes, their gear and tackle and trim." By my reckoning that includes glue guns and specialty scissors and all manner of glitter. What I particularly love about Hopkins is that his is not a generic celebration of God's awesomeness and wonder. He writes at an angle: turning the reader's eyes aslant, readjusting the frame, refocusing the viewfinder—choose your metaphor.

PIED BEAUTY

Glory be to God for dappled things–
    For skies of couple-colour as a brinded cow;
      For rose-moles all in stipple upon trout that swim;
Fresh-firecoal chestnut-falls; finches' wings;
    Landscape plotted and pieced—fold, fallow, and plough;
      And áll trádes, their gear and tackle and trim.

All things counter, original, spare, strange;
    Whatever is fickle, freckled (who knows how?)
      With swift, slow; sweet, sour; adazzle, dim;
He fathers-forth whose beauty is past change:
    Praise him.[7]

Here Hopkins wants us to look again at small, "patchy" things—
not a clichéd view of beauty in an unbroken, glossy aesthetic or a
grand symbol. No, he says: it's not just the cow, it's the variegated
colors of the cow; it's not just the fish, but its very spots; it's not just
the bird, but the bird's wing. The sublime can be found anywhere,
indeed everywhere, including the gorgeous quilt that is farmland.
Every job is lovely—and all the tools we need to do them too. In
short, beauty—however we find it and no matter how unconventional, norm-defying, odd—is all a minutely choreographed dance
of praise.

In other words, Hopkins makes the surprising point that abundance shows itself in the observation of many, many small things.
Pay attention, he says, God's plenitude lies in particularity.

And the only response is thanksgiving.

MRS. COKER'S CELEBRATION

Several years ago, I was in England, researching the life of a very
minor Modernist poet. I had dutifully made the rounds of libraries
far and wide, and finally, after about a month, I had arrived at the
very last one on my list. My reward when I was done was to be my
first trip to France with my brother, who lived in England at the
time. To be honest, I was only visiting that particular library out
of a sense of extreme scholarly thoroughness (I refuse to say obses-
siveness) and because the manuscripts in question involved eight
letters from the über-Modernist T. S. Eliot to my poet's sister. I
submitted my manuscript request to the librarian and waited at
my assigned carrel for the arrival of the letters and a quick morning's work. Instead, after half the morning had elapsed, the librarian appeared with a trolley, heavy-laden with scrapbooks. I
was sure he had brought me the wrong order. Where were my eight
measly letters?

"Oh no," he replied, "the letters are somewhere in these," motioning vaguely to the groaning trolley. "Good luck," he chirped, practically skipping back to his desk.

Though I was a bit flummoxed, I am not one to let a smirking librarian beat me, so I emphatically took the top scrapbook off the pile. I opened it gingerly—and to my surprise, discovered an amazing world. What I had before me was a small portion of the scrapbooks kept over the course of a lifetime by a woman named Margot Coker.

Born in 1898, Coker had decided in her teen years that she would never be a person given to diary-keeping. Yet, she wanted to record her life in some real and material way, and so, in 1913, she began her scrapbook, a project that would end up lasting until her death. As a scholar of women's history and literature, I found her collection fascinating. On the right-hand page of each spread was the ephemera of a twentieth-century upper-middle-class English-woman's life: a piece of rubber from the factory in which she worked during World War I, the speeding tickets she received in one of her county's first cars (and the accompanying newspaper articles chronicling her misadventures), playbills and menus, pictures and postcards, programs from gardening expositions and philanthropic meetings, and yes, letters from friends like T. S. Eliot.

But it was the left-hand page of each spread that made her scrap-books extraordinary. Without fail, on every single page in multiple volumes spread over sixty years, the caption that accompanied the ephemera began with the words, *To celebrate.*

To celebrate the good: "To celebrate going to Shamley Green [her family's home] to help Mappy [her mother] move into her new house." But to celebrate the bad as well: "To celebrate the disastrous picnic," or the caption with some get-well cards, "To celebrate being stricken with shingles & what a foul disease."

Coker's playful sensibility of celebration was infectious. Indeed, I was so captivated that my trip to France was delayed, and I spent the next week and a half, from the time the library opened until it closed each evening, going through these self-titled "Celebration Books" from beginning to end. Here was a woman even less well-known than her minor-league sister, living a relatively typical existence for a woman of her class, and yet her life was one of the richest I have ever encountered.

As I progressed from year to year in the scrapbooks, I was utterly charmed by someone who deliberately worked to frame everything in such joyful terms, and I could imagine why people like Eliot enjoyed her hospitality so very much. As I reluctantly reached the last volume, I was genuinely sad over the death of a woman I had never met.

I wondered even then, *How would our lives as Christians be different if we were willing to more purposefully adopt Coker's model—a deliberate, daily orientation toward celebration?* After all, Psalm 145 calls for one generation to "commend" and "celebrate God's abundant goodness" to another. Are we doing that? Are we listening for it in what our literary ancestors are telling us?

Coker may have produced an outward embodiment of her inward spirit in the making of her scrapbooks. Or maybe her deliberate scrapbooking helped produce the celebration that she wanted to cultivate. Probably some combination thereof. But the relationship between attitude and action being manifested in something—a little like Hopkins's instress and inscape coming together to testify to God's working in each life—seems like a good model.

The summer of my junior year in high school provides, perhaps, another example. It was the summer we spent cleaning out my grandmother's house. My Grandmother Kline was a lifelong resident of Des Moines. Her house had been built in the late 1920s by my grandfather on land that she had won in a dancing contest (a subject for a whole other book, obviously). Like most Midwestern homes of that era, it wasn't a large house, though it did have an attic and a basement. But sixty years on, it was well-filled with a lifetime's worth of stuff. My grandmother had been quite the clothes-horse, and she had carefully lined the rafters of the attic with her wardrobe. She'd worked for Meredith Publishing (home of *Better Homes and Gardens*) for some twenty years, and she'd kept many of their early publications, neatly tied with string in her attic. She'd canned fruits and vegetables, jellies and jams every year, and a small room in the basement was filled with her products. Most of all, as I shared in chapter one, my grandmother was an inveterate reader and book collector—so every room in the house featured bookcases. And thousands of books.

Sixty years of stuff would have been bad enough. But because she had grown ill, she had come to live with us in New Mexico, and so the house had sat empty for many months. Eventually the task could be put off no longer. As an only child, my mother had no one else to help her, except for me and my brother and sister. So off we went.

It was unpleasant work, to be sure: the Iowa summer was unremittingly sultry; the hot and sticky air amplified by the close, un-air-conditioned atmosphere in the house. After months of being shut up, dust was everywhere. It was hard, tiring work, sorting and packing and toting trash to the curb. Worst of all, the shower stopped working soon after we arrived. The plumber didn't seem to think we were much of a priority, so we made do with baths as well as we could.

Yet, my siblings and I often talk about this summer with great fondness.

Here's why: we got to eat out a lot that summer—and at every restaurant, our mother let us order an appetizer. This was, in itself, a big deal. But my mother made it into something more: we kept a running comparison going all summer of the many kinds of onion rings available in the restaurants of Des Moines. (You might be surprised, actually, at the varieties available.) Dorky? Probably. But it was also a silly, fun thing—something we looked forward to at every meal, something we still talk about when we remember our mother, now gone these many years. It makes me think of the proverb that reminds us, "Better a small serving of vegetables with love / than a fattened ox with hatred" (Prov 15:17). There's enough goodness around that it doesn't take much to be reminded of it. Sometimes it just takes an onion ring.

Scrapbooks and onion rings, even in superabundance, are perhaps little to show for a life. Yet they are undeniable witnesses to the heart of the gospel—and one of the scandals of the cross: God's lavish gesture of love. It seems to me that we don't think often enough about the extravagance of grace. Indeed, I would wager that we have heard more sermons on stewardship than on extravagance. We "make do," emotionally and spiritually, fearful of giving ourselves away, fearful of not having quite enough. We think that frugality means only ever holding back—we typically do not mean spending wisely. We focus on our finitude rather than God's infinity.

But in the sixteenth century, *extravagant* was a noun meaning someone who roamed far outside of prescribed limits. As such, the word suggests to me something very rich, indeed: going out of our way as a habit of heart and mind. Is such a gesture ever wasted? Mrs. Coker would have found something to celebrate in adopting this original meaning of extravagance—and, as those who believe in the excess of God's grace, perhaps we should be less afraid to do the same.

SLOW LOOKING AND TAKING OFF ONE'S SHOES

This chapter begins with an excerpt from the Victorian poet Elizabeth Barrett Browning's epic poem *Aurora Leigh*:

Earth's crammed with heaven
and every common bush afire with God
But only he who sees, takes off his shoes.

Like Hopkins in "Pied Beauty," Barrett Browning is calling us to notice the pervasiveness of God: the heavenly presence isn't lightly sprinkled or rare, it is "crammed," overflowing. "*Every common bush*" is on fire—not just a select few. But the third line is the most interesting: "But only he who sees, takes off his shoes." Note the implication: there are those who do not see these wildfires burning all around them. Instead we are, as another nineteenth-century poet, Matthew Arnold, puts it, befuddled by the "thousand nothings of the hour."[8] The consequence of inattention is that, as Elizabeth Barrett Browning points out, we miss not just the wonder of God's plenitude but the chance to respond appropriately by reorienting ourselves into a place of worship and gratitude. Gratitude requires paying attention to all the things over which we have absolutely no understanding or control (which—let's be honest—is almost everything). I don't think we consider often enough how legitimately weird it must have been for Moses to witness the sight of a bush on fire. But to notice these things, to understand their source, and to say thank you for them means we acknowledge that we can't do it all, that we haven't done it all, that we reject what Barbara Brown Taylor has called "the idolatry of omnicompetence."[9] Sounds a lot like resisting the call back to Egypt.

We often lament our inattentiveness—but what is to be done to cultivate it? I decided to reorient my first-year composition class: instead of plunging directly into all things thesis-driven, I decided to spend the first two weeks with the class learning and then practicing "slow looking" techniques. Much like the "slow food" movement, slow looking, based in part on the work of Shari Tishman, "simply means taking the time to carefully observe more than meets the eye at first glance." It's not just that we miss a great deal with our rushing and inattention, but we don't know how to look deeper, even if we wanted to. Thus, Tishman argues that "slow looking" is a "learnable practice."[10] Importantly, while the concept does ask for a deliberate difference in pace, slow looking isn't about noticing everything—an obvious impossibility. Instead, it is about acquiring tools to see more and to be cognizant of how we are seeing. It's about being more attentive but also more attuned to what you are seeing and what that says, too (about what you notice and why).

We started the class with students taking photos of each other from an unusual angle—photos we later analyzed in class alongside their official university ID photos, asking how each picture caused us to see and re-see each other, and how each caused us to consider what assumptions and allusions we brought to our looking. We spent a class period outside in our nature preserve testing our lateral and vertical vision, the effects of stillness and motion, and insights from scale and scope. Students walked alone in the cold silence for fifteen minutes and stood still for two minutes in the middle of that time—noting what they observed in both states. Another class period found us in our Center Art Gallery, each of us selecting a picture and then generating as many questions as we could after observing it for some minutes. Then we selected another picture and exhaustively inventoried every possible element. Finally, students sat in silence in front of yet another painting—for fifteen minutes (a huge challenge, which they passed with nary a look at their phones)—and then wrote about how their perceptions changed from first look to long look. In yet another class period, we spent time disassembling a book to understand it by deconstruction—and then did the same with an abstract concept.

To bring it all together, we read an excerpt from Alexandra Horowitz's *On Looking: A Walker's Guide to the Art of Observation*.

In the book, Horowitz chronicles walks she took around her New York neighborhood with various experts, discovering what only they could make visible.[11] As the final activity, my students, too, took a walk across campus, following a route I gave them. They made use of the techniques we'd been practicing and identified areas where they are emerging experts. The resulting initial drafts were lovely. Richly detailed, deeply thoughtful, and wonderfully self-reflective. In only two weeks, it was almost staggering how much progress they had already made. It turns out there are ways we might help each other see more fully. The best thing, though, is the papers' sometimes-articulated, but always underlying, sense of gratitude. For seeing more around them and inside them. For the affirmation that in a shattered world the fragment of seeing that they bring makes the mosaic a little more complete, a little more beautiful. For the God who gives us so much to see and so many people to see it all with.

SISTER LEO'S COOKIES

Every morning among all my email is a small gem: a blessing from the Dominican Sisters of Grand Rapids. Mostly penned by Maxine Shonk, OP, the blessings focus on a characteristic of God and how that part of God's multitudinous character models and transforms us. During some parts of the year, email subscribers to these blessings also receive stories about Dominican sisters who have reached milestones in their ministries, stories that chronicle the ways in which God has worked in equally multitudinous ways through these religious women.

One of my favorite stories is about Sister Leo Mergener, who worked in a children's home in the 1940s and 1950s. She was chastised for giving the children too many cookies and told to limit them to only one a day. In response, Sister Leo began baking the biggest possible cookies she could. As per instructions, the children only received one daily cookie—but what a cookie it was!

I love the spirit of Sister Leo's cookies: the way they proclaim the abundant life, the way they insist that God's extravagant love finds tangible expressions in the way we interact with and serve one other. My mother would have found a kindred spirit in Sister Leo. She took unapologetic delight in celebrating events, big and small. In her unwavering gestures of hospitality, I witnessed the truth of William Blake's claim that "exuberance is beauty." When as typical teenagers my siblings and I would groan over her effusive (to us) declarations of "I love you," she would reply, "I don't want you to have any doubts." She remembered little things that people mentioned, and she had a gift closet full of what she'd tracked down and was saving for just the right moment. And a never-ending supply of cards, for every occasion. Pace the television show *Parks & Rec*, she was the original queen of "treat yourself," a great permission giver for raucous extravagance. My mother was only a little older than I am now when she died at age fifty-five. Now, over twenty years later, it's quite difficult to imagine that she would have been nearing eighty.

But the older I have gotten, the more I have recognized the anxieties that led her to always identify 1 Peter 5:7, "Cast all your cares upon him for he cares for you" (KJV), as her favorite verse. She experienced the death of her father when she was only nine, suffered two devastating miscarriages, survived a husband away at war after she had just had her first baby, and oversaw multiple moves across the globe. She had to establish a home (often in less-than-ideal circumstances), make friends and find a new community, and help her children navigate the whole thing. Again and again over the nine times we moved during my childhood (and she had done it for some years before my birth).

I thought of her often during the pandemic and considered how she would have responded. I'm sure she would have laughed and cooked and found silly ways to put everyone at ease. But she would have done all of that even as she prayed and planned and probably worried that all would be well. The day she died, she taught a Bible study on God's providence, where she told some of the events of her life that I shared above. As she finished the lesson, she told the gathered women, "Whatever happens today, remember to put your weight down on the goodness of God." Just hours later, a brain aneurysm ended her life.

I love the acknowledgment implied in that "whatever happens": it means that "whatever" will indeed happen. But it's not the only thing. The care of God means there is so much more. During the pandemic lockdown, a friend wrote me these lovely words: "There is so much that physical separation requires of us. And so much to which solitude invites us." Just so.

When I graduated from college, my parents hosted a party for me—at which thirteen cakes appeared. I don't think thirteen cakes was the original plan. My mother's initial concept for the party was something simple and welcoming: in her words, sandwiches, "finger food," and cake, all served in the comfort of our house and backyard. Her idea was to let people choose from several cakes (because people should always have a choice), and as those were finished, to bring out several more—a never-ending rotation of baked hospitality. My mother was a major proponent (and a living embodiment) of what she often urged me to cultivate as I was growing up: "a kind and gracious spirit." So, somehow (and I think her friends brought a few to "help"), the thirteen cakes materialized. And although many people attended the party, we did, needless to say, have quite a bit of cake left over.

My mother didn't care, offering one of her trademark comments: "It's always better to offer too much than too little." Leftovers again—

those little reminders of gracious abundance! Less than a decade later when she died, her hospitality was one of her qualities most frequently evoked. In fact, at her visitation, the first words from one of my friends were, "I still remember those thirteen cakes." The flip side is that abundance without action is waste. About a year after my mother died, I faced a task that proved much harder than I had anticipated: I spent an afternoon cleaning out her standing freezer. She had fully stocked it only days before her death, in anticipation of all the meals she would prepare. In the year that followed, my father had rarely, if ever, opened it. Instead, I stood that day in the cold garage and took each piece of meat, now brown and freezer-burned, and placed them in garbage bags, reminded of what she would never do again. All that food, all those meals, so much a part of my mother's generous spirit—gone. Those things that could have nourished someone, ruined and beyond using.

And isn't the same thing true of the abundance of our own lives? Perhaps we are commanded to love God and each other with all our heart and soul and mind and strength because we need to be reminded that such love requires a full-on commitment with every part of our being, bringing a generosity of spirit to every sphere and every interaction: the emotional, the spiritual, the intellectual, the physical. Because God knows that if we don't, the magnitude of that sad and sorry waste will be very great, indeed: a freezer-burned life.

IMMORTAL DIAMONDS

We believe in a God who not only feeds the multitudes but makes sure there are leftovers. There's always enough. But maybe acknowledging a generous God is easier than seeing ourselves as worthy of God's lavish love. We don't want to view our worthiness through the lens of the "prosperity gospel" or "toxic positivity," concepts that historian Kate Bowler has so effectively called out in her studies

Blessed: A History of the American Prosperity Gospel and *Everything Happens for a Reason*.[12] We are not entitled to and not deserving of God's love but worthy, nevertheless. Think about how hard it is for many people to receive even a compliment. As I ask at the chapter's opening, what if the stories we tell about God and about ourselves proceed from our absolute conviction of God's loving generosity *and* our own "enoughness"?

I'll answer that by ending with another poem by Gerard Manley Hopkins, "That Nature Is a Heraclitean Fire and of the Comfort of the Resurrection."[13] That title can seem a little daunting, and the poem itself can appear almost indecipherable on first approach. But it provides one of the most powerful articulations of our inherent worthiness before God found anywhere in literature.

The poem begins in the clouds as a storm develops. Soon, the rain is heavily falling, and the trees are shaken by the wind. In the aftermath of the dramatic storm, the speaker notices how the ground has been changed by it, how much has been erased from the surface of the earth. But unlike "Pied Beauty," which moves toward praise, here the speaker begins to spiral into despair: not only is the surface of the earth changeable, our very footprints easily erased, but nothing is permanent. Referencing the pre-Socratic philosopher Heraclitus, who believed the condition of the world tended toward fire,[14] the speaker of "That Nature" grows more and more despondent with each line as he thinks of the world and all human accomplishments being nothing beyond a great trash heap, headed for flaming destruction. Finally, reaching the bottom of his grief, he cries out, "O pity and indignation!" as he realizes that no

mark

Is any of him at all so stark

But vastness blurs and time beats level.

In other words, even the person who leaves the most dramatic mark on the world will still eventually have their memory rubbed out and be forgotten, just like the rain erases the ruts in the ground. If it's all going to burn up anyway and nothing a person is or does matters, feeling sorrow, anger, and depression seems about right. What's the point?

But here the poem takes an amazing turn, as the speaker exclaims "Enough!" Hopkins is renowned for his wordplay—and though the first use of "enough" is to stop the descent into existential crisis, it is also the thesis word for the rest of the poem. Why are we enough? Because of Christ's "enoughness" in the resurrection—what the poet calls "a heart's clarion." The resurrection, then, is a wake-up call, a guiding light—even to a ship that is "foundering" in despair and going down.

What's more, as the speaker begins to meditate on the power of the resurrection, he not only begins to see the power and the plenitude of God as manifested in that mighty act but also the eschatological vision that the resurrection makes possible. The fact of the resurrection changes his view of human beings, himself included. Here's how the poem ends:

In a flash, at a trumpet crash,

I am all at once what Christ is, | since he was what I am, and

This Jack, joke, poor potsherd, | patch, matchwood,
immortal diamond,

Is immortal diamond.

Notice that enoughness doesn't mean perfect or good. Hopkins acknowledges that much of us is broken, perishable, lamentable, a "joke." But even now, Hopkins asserts, we are also already "immortal diamonds." Precious, entirely precious, a jewel of great price. Worth redeeming.

And even if Heraclitus is right and the condition of the world is fire, it is the perishable that will be burned away, but our essential identity, our immortal-diamondness will last forever. Diamonds can survive any fire.

Can we see ourselves as immortal diamonds? Already beautiful, already valuable, already beloved of a God for whom plenitude lives in particularity and for whom there is always enough for everyone? Let us open wide our hands to receive and to give. That is a story worth telling.

3

Graced with the Ordinary

Holy is the dish and drain
The soap and sink,
and the cup and plate
And the warm wool socks,
and the cold white tile

Shower heads and good dry towels
And frying eggs sound like psalms
With bits of salt measured in my palm
It's all a part of a sacrament
As holy as a day is spent. . . .

Holy is the place I stand
To give whatever small good I can
And the empty page, and the open book
Redemption everywhere I look

CARRIE NEWCOMER,
"HOLY AS A DAY IS SPENT"

MY VERY FAVORITE NOVEL is George Eliot's *Middlemarch*.[1] It's a novel Virginia Woolf famously said was "one of the few English novels written for grownup people,"[2] by which I think she meant that it's a book that struggles with all the dilemmas and disappointment of adulthood. Most of the marriages in the book take place early on, for example, and the plot follows these couples into the problems that come with everyday life together. Other strands of the plot focus on professional ambition, small-town politics, and finding one's way into meaningful work—and all the choices and complications, compromises and consequences (intended and unintended) that come along with all of it. One of the leading characters is the young Dorothea Brooke, who begins the novel yearning to live an epic life of service, to be a new Saint Teresa, the sixteenth century saint who, Eliot explains, "found her epos in the reform of a religious order."[3] Over the course of the novel, Dorothea finds that such a life is not available to her, even as she works diligently for the good of others. In the book's moving final paragraph, Eliot observes of Dorothea:

> Her full nature, like that river of which Cyrus broke the strength, spent itself in channels which had no great name on the earth. But the effect of her being on those around her was incalculably diffusive: for the growing good of the world is partly dependent on unhistoric acts; and that things are not so ill with you and me as they might have been, is half owing to the number who lived faithfully a hidden life, and rest in unvisited tombs.[4]

This emphasis on "unhistoric acts," on "liv[ing] faithfully a hidden life," then, offers a different narrative paradigm than the one about Saint Teresa that opens the book. It's fascinating to think that the classical literary form traditionally most admired is the epic— Homer's *Iliad* and *Odyssey*, Virgil's *Aeneid*. Big stories, big adventures, big heroes. By contrast, *Middlemarch* is also a massive work, but its length, Eliot implies, is necessary to capture even the most ordinary people and their most ordinary lives. In other words, everyone's life could fill volumes, if attended to properly. And one of the lessons of *Middlemarch* is that we need to do just that—and come to value the influence of faithful people doing good. While we may think we yearn, like Dorothea at the book's opening, for the sweeping saga and the grand drama, we come to understand that there's another measure of success possible.

In the last chapter, I argued that plenitude lies in particularity. That is, rather than think of abundance as only epic events and large-scale productions, I asked us to pay attention to the small instances of God's generosity happening everywhere. This chapter asks us to consider those small instances over time—that is, looking for the faithful quotidian as another important characteristic of the nourishing narratives we are seeking to tell about God and our-selves. After all, that's the way of the Scripture: sure, the Bible has a great, overarching story of creation to consummation, but it is made up of many small, deeply personal stories, testifying to God's faithfulness, generation to generation. Faithfulness, as the hymn says, "morning by morning." Kathleen Norris's *The Quotidian Mysteries*, Julie Canlis's *A Theology of the Ordinary*, and Tish Harrison Warren's *Liturgy of the Ordinary* each provide excellent introductions to the theological imperatives of the everyday. And these are stories worth looking for and telling.

For me, one gorgeous example of this comes in the song from which I've taken the epigraph for this chapter: "Holy as a Day Is Spent" by the wonderful singer-songwriter Carrie Newcomer. In this song, Newcomer catalogs a list of the activities and people she encounters through the day, each leading her to "redemption every-where [she] looks." Mary Oliver's poetry has a similar focus. Though we might be more familiar with her well-known poem "The Summer's Day"[5]—with its invitation to relishing one's "one wild and precious life"—much of our lives are lived in ordinary time, so a better frame might be Oliver's "Summer Morning" and its vision of a light-filled world, full of sometimes difficult things:

Heart,

I implore you,

it's time to come back

from the dark,

it's morning,

the hills are pink

and the roses

whatever they felt

in the valley of the night

are opening now

their soft dresses,

their leaves

are shining.

Why are you laggard?

Sure you have seen this

a thousand times,

which isn't half enough.

Let the world

have its way with you,

luminous as it is

with mystery

and pain—

graced as it is

with the ordinary.[6]

In this poem, Oliver reminds us that seeing something "a thousand times" does not make it any less worthy or less worth examining yet again. Oliver's morning is "luminous" with both "mystery and pain"—but that itself is part of the ordinary—that is, what we should expect. Instead, even in the one thousandth iteration, in the one thousandth look, there is still more to see, more to learn from, more to love and lament, more to mourn and celebrate.

TECHNOLOGIES OF LOOKING

One challenge, though, is figuring out how to really see the already looked at. We're now on the other side of the centennial commemorations of the "Great War" that took place during the 2010s, culminating in 2018's Armistice Day remembrances, such as the particularly moving tribute featuring millions of poppies cascading around the Tower of London. Maybe unusually, World War I never felt that far away to me—as a military brat, the horse-drawn caissons of WWI often came out on parade or were fired for ceremonial occasions on the base (and, as long as I can remember, I've known the words to the Army song that proudly describes the caissons "rolling along"). It also was a war that in my childhood was a living memory for my grandparents, all born right around the turn of the twentieth century. So I remember as a little girl, my grandmother, for example, telling me of going down to the train station with a huge crowd to send off the first wave of boys in 1917.

Familiar or not, WWI had such profound effects on everything that followed—and though we've all heard about the war, what do we actually know about the events? One of my classroom solutions thus far has been that each time I teach my nineteenth- and twentieth-century British literature survey course, I include a unit on the WWI poets, such as Wilfred Owen, Siegfried Sassoon, and Rupert Brooke. I tell of the nine million combatants killed, of the ruinous trenches, of the introduction through chemical and biological warfare of more horrific forms of destruction than had ever before been seen. My students typically have only basic knowledge of the war from high school history, though they are soon horrified by these fuller descriptions. We talk, too, about all the ways that war continues to be glorified in contemporary media, while the cost is not always accurately described or understood.

Certainly, poetry helps get at the emotions of those who served. But Peter Jackson, who is best known as the director of the Lord of the Rings films, made a documentary called *They Shall Not Grow Old* that takes reenvisioning to a different level.[7] The film, whose title is taken from Laurence Binyon's 1914 poem "For the Fallen," chronicles the life of the average British infantry soldier over the course of WWI. It is stunning—and I use that word with all its variety of meanings.

Indeed, it is almost impossible to praise the technical "wow" of the film too highly. Commissioned by London's Imperial War Museum (worth a visit, if you are ever in London), the film uses only the one hundred hours of footage held at the museum. No new footage was shot. And there is no narrator nor talking head: all the voices are WWI veterans interviewed in the 1960s and 1970s. The film is a marvel to look at: the speeds have all been regularized so that everyone moves in a natural way. When colorization kicks in partway into the film, the attention to detail is astounding. Jackson obsessed over getting everything right, down to visiting locations to match the color of the grass or researching the correct shade of the blue in a soldier's uniform patch. Even more amazing to me was the sound design for the formerly silent films: the guns you hear are accurate to those at the time, for instance. Moreover, Jackson hired lip readers to discover what the men are saying and had actors dub in the lines (with appropriate regional accents), so that the viewer has an incredibly intense impression of the life of these men.

Some critics, however, have objected to the colorization—some for issues of purity (it wasn't colored then, so it shouldn't be colored now), others for issues of aesthetics. Following the credits, Jackson includes a thirty-minute technical "making-of" discussion in which he addresses some of these concerns. But my defense of the technique is a pedagogical one. Yes, the film is very intense—so intense I sometimes had to look away. But therein is its effectiveness. The men of Jackson's documentary are not grainy, herky-jerky shadows of the past; instead, they are living, breathing men who look like your father, brother, or friend. The formerly muted tones of the hellish trenches and the devastating wastelands come alive in all their visceral horror. And the immediacy is shocking: you feel like you are watching a movie made yesterday. In portraying the daily life alongside the hostilities over four long years, Jackson's vibrant film does us a great service by restoring the humanity of these men's lives, reminding us that shadows don't fight wars, and that war is neither detached from real life nor aesthetically pleasing. In its chronicling of everyday life, a narrative emerges at odds with so many Hollywood depictions of the sweeping glory of battle. Both in subject and in style, *They Shall Not Grow Old* provides a way of more richly seeing something—with more detail, more verisimilitude—in order to expand our vision.

I wonder what color and sound we need to enrich our reading of Scripture, especially when it begins to feel gray and washed out and rather silent in what it says to us? When the people of the Bible feel distant? Perhaps that comes through reading a different translation, perhaps through interacting with a complementary piece of art or literature or film, perhaps through receiving insights from a sermon or worship experience in song or dance. Optimally, over a lifetime, it comes through all of these. Because faithful reading is not a one-time occurrence, after all, but a lifetime conversation with centuries of readers and with our Author and Finisher too.

IN THE STORM

Sometimes rather than a deepening of detail, faithful reading requires a defamiliarizing of the ordinary to see it anew. Here, another of Mary Oliver's poems, "In the Storm,"[8] has been enormously helpful to me.

The seaside scene the poem opens on is a tumultuous one. It's hostile and bitterly cold. Ducks are being covered up by the snow. It's a world that's bleak and unwelcoming.

> Some black ducks
> were shrugged up
> on the shore.
> It was snowing
>
> hard, from the east,
> and the sea
> was in disorder.

And yet, Oliver then provides a tender image of the ducks huddling together against the storm, giving warmth to each other. In their coming together, too, they not only help each other survive but are able to offer a kind of anatine hospitality to some smaller birds.

Then some sanderlings,

five inches long
with beaks like wire,
flew in,
snowflakes on their backs,

and settled
in a row
behind the ducks—
whose backs were also

covered with snow—
so close
they were all but touching,
they were all but under

the roof of the ducks' tails,
so the wind, pretty much,
blew over them.
They stayed that way, motionless,

for maybe an hour,
then the sanderlings,
each a handful of feathers,
shifted, and were blown away

out over the water,
which was still raging.
But, somehow,
they came back

and again the ducks,
like a feathered hedge,
let them
stoop there, and live.

This "feathered hedge" of the ducks that shelter these little sanderlings doesn't just protect them once, but again and again as the sanderlings are blown out to sea and then fight their way back. Of course, the protection the ducks offer (which Oliver delicately refers to as under the "roof of their tails") is nothing glamorous. But it is enough. More than enough, really, since allowing the sanderlings to "stoop there" under the ducks' bottoms lets them live.

Oliver makes us question whether this scene is a miracle, a word that has its roots in the classical Latin *mīrāculum*,[9] or "object of wonder":

If someone you didn't know
told you this,
as I am telling you this,
would you believe it?

Belief isn't always easy.
But this much I have learned,
if not enough else—
to live with my eyes open.

I know what everyone wants
is a miracle.
This wasn't a miracle.
Unless, of course, kindness—

as now and again
some rare person has suggested—
is a miracle.
As surely it is.

The answer is clear: though "belief isn't always easy," but, at a minimum, if we learn to "live with . . . eyes open" we can discern miracles in kindness—even if it seems unspectacular. Oliver's poem urges us toward all the testimonies of grace that continually surround us. But we need to recognize them.

And we need to have more unglamorous stories, like Oliver's. Some years ago, a non-Christian friend put an item on Facebook that made me pause. The post was quoting the comedian Hannibal Buress's internet meme, riffing on people saying to him, "I'll pray for you":

> I don't like it when people say I'll pray for you. "I'll pray for you, I'll pray for you." You're gonna pray for me? So basically you're gonna sit at home and do nothing? Because that's what your prayers are. You're doing nothing while I'm struggling with a situation. So don't pray for me: make me a sandwich or something. 'Cause I'm very upset right now and I can't make my own sandwiches, so that would be cool if you made me a sandwich instead of praying. That's very lazy.[10]

On top of Buress' comments, my friend titled her post, "Sometimes I Just Need a Sandwich," which struck me as about as clear an articulation as one can get for the absolute necessity for us to be, as Barbara Brown Taylor has put it, "God's sign language" in all that we do. Instead, how often we easily lapse into God talk, how often a pious platitude comes to our lips.[11] And how often that is accompanied by a failure to embody our faith, by a failure to live out the words of Matthew 25 about offering food and drink and shelter and clothes (Mt 25:31-46).

It can't be all sandwich making, naturally, and I am certainly all for a robust theologically informed praxis, but I appreciated the reminder that daily kindnesses are powerful witnesses. Christians know that, of course—you will know them by their fruit and all that. But I wonder how often my friend had received what sounded to her like empty words when an apple—literally—might have been more welcome. Oliver's poem reminds us that in our own huddling together, we also need to welcome our fellow sufferers who battle the elements too.

And the poem's best reassurance is that this welcome needn't be fancy—just dependable. Or put another way: What small, unglamorous kindnesses could we offer as shelter to those we encounter?

Of course, ducks' butts aren't the only place of shelter, and I'm certainly not arguing that we should only seek solace in the unbeautiful. My friend Jane Zwart has a gorgeous poem, "On Beauty and Being Just,"[12] where the speaker reminds herself that delighting in the "flamboyants" can lead us to insight too:

It is possible that I have been unfair
to them, the flamboyants:
to opals, to abalones, to moths
more phosphorescent
than any eyeshadow I've worn—
because who knows?

Maybe the painted bunting
would willingly trade
his layered, paint-by-number capes
for the robin's rusty apron. Maybe
the hibiscus is not a satellite dish
tilting on its stem to overhear
the praise of passers-by
but an umbrella mortified
that day has left it open
in a narrow place to dry. Maybe
the Northern Lights' magic
is static, escaped photons
from the cupped palm of a modest
earth, smoothing her skirt.

. . .

But there, too, I have been unjust,
asking the bird to disavow
his jaunty beauty, rose mallow to flower
rue. Wanting to be fair—

let me trade it for plain
delight. Let me quit shaming
the flame-like things
or, at least, let the wind
unwinding its argon sarong
not mind the likes of me.

After all, the *Oxford English Dictionary* also speaks of miracle as an "astonishing thing." How might we astonish each other with kindness, wherever we find it, whether mundane or exotic? How could such behavior change the narrative for those who watch for what Christians consistently do, not what they say?

SEEDS OF JOY

We know instinctually how important small acts, consistently performed, can be—for good or for ill. To return to George Eliot's *Middlemarch*: Partway into the novel, Eliot presents a scene where Dorothea and her husband, the dried-up, pedantic scholar Edward Casaubon, have an argument. In the aftermath, to begin to make amends Dorothea tries to take her husband's arm, and he responds by "k[eeping] his hands behind him and allow[ing] her pliant arm to cling with difficulty against his rigid arm."[13] A seeming insignificance. But no, says Eliot, "it is in these acts called trivialities that the seeds of joy are forever wasted, until men and women look round with haggard faces at the devastation their own waste has made, and say, the earth bears no harvest of sweetness—calling their denial knowledge."[14]

We fail, Eliot argues, when we do not see the influence of every possible act of kindness, when we do not cultivate the "seeds of joy" that are within our power to plant in the lives of those around us. A cultivation that takes time and care and patience—daily work to bring something to fruition. And when we later bemoan the emotionally sterile landscape we inhabit, we are only deceiving ourselves as to how we arrived there (and the faithful work we avoided).

But what about stories where those "seeds of joy" *are* planted?

While Nobel Peace Prize–winner Aung San Suu Kyi was under house arrest for years, heavily guarded and deeply isolated, separated from her husband and children, she often found solace in a dilapidated piano (even if that solace came in sometimes angrily pounding the keys). She played Pachelbel, Bach, Mozart, Telemann—a small thing, no doubt, given the rest of her circumstances. But that one freedom—the freedom that comes from the hope that art and beauty can provide—nourished the strength to pursue the greater freedoms for her country for which Suu Kyi yearned. The piano was one thing the generals of Myanmar were not bold enough to remove during her imprisonment.

But here's what really struck me about this story: It is not just that Suu Kyi played. It is not just that the music gave her, perhaps, a significant edge in the psychological war she waged while under arrest. It's not really a story about Suu Kyi at all. It was that she was *able* to play because of the work of three men—Saw Simon, Ko Paul, and Saw Sheperd.

Piano tuners.

As the *Los Angeles Times* reported, over the course of Suu Kyi's many years of confinement, these three men worked (often under intense surveillance themselves) to maintain an instrument ravaged by the vicissitudes of a tropical climate.[15] It wasn't easy—the instrument was old and the spare parts hard to find. But they managed to keep the instrument playable. A small act of resistance. One wonders how much more difficult it would have been for Suu Kyi to survive and emerge from prison without her music, only made possible by these men's efforts. Surely, whatever one makes of Suu Kyi's extremely mixed record as the leader of Myanmar post-imprisonment, when the history of the quest for democracy in Myanmar is written, Simon, Paul, and Sheperd will deserve credit for their unwavering acts of opposition.

Or perhaps a less dramatic example.

You have probably seen the famous photo of a high school-aged Bill Clinton meeting President John F. Kennedy. In the photo, you see Clinton (and the boys around him) wearing polo shirts with the emblem "Boys Nation," a mock government and civics program that has been run by the American Legion since 1946. Boys Nation is the follow-up program of Boys State, where rising high school seniors are competitively selected and then sent for weeklong participation in elections at every level (city, county, state), in governing exercises, and in drafting and debating legislation. State politicians and community leaders visit to lecture and inspire. At the conclusion of the week, the entire "state" gathers and elects two senators to send to Washington, DC, for an additional, all-expenses-paid week of mock government at the federal level. In Washington, not only do "senators" meet their actual senators and representatives, debate legislation, run a presidential election (between the Nationalists and the Federalists), and shadow officials who mirror their own mock appointments, but they also are taken to all the major monuments and museums.

Most importantly, they get a Rose Garden ceremony with the president.

Well, except in my year.

In 1985, I was selected by my Girls State peers to attend Girls Nation (the female equivalent of Boys Nation), run by the American Legion Auxiliary. Girls Nation was truly amazing, and it made my first time in Washington magical. I rode with my representative on the underground train to the House floor to vote with him; I got to sit behind one of my senators, chair of the appropriations committee, in a hearing; I spent an entire morning with the treasurer of the US (also from my state); and much, much more.

But in the summer of 1985, Ronald Reagan had surgery. Boys Nation got to meet him, but we girls were out of luck. They tried to give us an extra nice White House tour, but it just wasn't the same. No Rose Garden, no presidential photo. Major disappointment all around.

Nevertheless, we were still having incredible opportunities, such as being taken to a performance at the Kennedy Center on our penultimate evening to see the phenomenal Loretta Lynn. During the show's intermission, I began looking around. We were massive political junkies and during our time we had spotted lots of famous politicians. I wondered if anyone else might be in the audience. Looking up to the balcony, I thought I spotted the vice president and said to a friend, "Hey, isn't that George Bush?"

"I don't know," she said, "but that white-haired woman is definitely Barbara."

Naturally, I decided we had to go up and try to meet him. Most of the other girls were skeptical, but a hearty band of about eight followed me up the stairs. Now the American Legion Auxiliary ladies—and they *were* ladies—required us to wear dresses almost all the time. Dresses to which were affixed long ribbon-y things that said "Girls Nation," topped with a button with our state's name. In this getup I approached one of the Secret Service agents and told him our tale of woe: how we didn't get to meet Reagan or see the Rose Garden—and couldn't we please meet Vice President Bush. The Secret Service guy gamely said he couldn't promise anything, but he'd go check.

The intermission wore on, and the Secret Service guy never came back. Half the girls gave up. The lights warning of the intermission's conclusion began to flicker.

And then, just as we were turning around to go back to our seats, the door to the balcony opened and the Secret Service lined up on either side to reveal Vice President George H. W. Bush himself. In a pre-selfie age, I didn't get a picture with him (though, while he was talking to us, I did take a badly focused picture with a little disposable camera), but the image is one I've never forgotten. He greeted us enthusiastically, never seeming like we were imposing on his evening. Mostly, I remember how interested he was in each of us. How unhurriedly he spoke to us together and then in turn. How he commiserated with us about not getting to go to the White House. He apologized that Barbara had needed to stay with their guests (even while telling us everyone else who was in the box). As he learned where we were from, he offered tidbits that he knew about each place, making each one of us feel like our hometown was known and appreciated. He was genuinely warm. For five teenage girls, it was the highlight of the entire trip.

This experience came to mind when Bush died in 2018. Like all of us, his legacy is complicated, and he has already become the subject of what Frank Bruni in the *New York Times* called the "obituary wars," where "we like our villains without redemption and our heroes without blemish, and we frequently assign those roles in overly strict alignment with our ideology."[16] Bruni goes on to argue that "we do seem to be getting worse at complexity. At nuance. At allowing for the degree to which virtue and vice commingle in most people, including our leaders, and at understanding that it's not a sign of softness to summon some respect for someone with a contrary viewpoint and a history of mistakes. It's a sign of maturity. And it just might be a path back to a better place."[17]

Part of nuance, part of complexity, part of that "path back to a better place" is telling as much of the story as we can. I think that too often translates, however, to telling as much of the bad part of the story as we can. And there's always plenty of that in all our stories.

So we need to say it: good and bad. I want to make sure, though, to acknowledge the part that was good, that was noble, that was generous. This doesn't mean erasing or ignoring negative actions or traits, but it does mean that in the telling of a president's life, his making time to say hello to a teenage girl and her geeky government friends does rate. It is a small thing—a seed—but it was planted. William Wordsworth declares in "Tintern Abbey" that the "best portion of a good man's life" is "his little, nameless, unremembered, acts / Of kindness and of love."[18] For me, this little act of kindness so long ago is not yet unremembered.

Maybe one more example, closer to home.

When I was a child, I never had any trouble believing in an absolutely loving God because I figured that if God were even half as amazing as my dad, everything would be fine. To be honest, I probably believe that still, even as I know it probably skates some kind of line of appropriate reverence.

Or maybe it doesn't. My father would be the very first to acknowledge his limitations, but I do think that, as even an imperfect image bearer, he has lived a life of constancy that gives praise to the God he serves.

My father is now in his eighties, and it's still difficult to find words to celebrate the life of a good man. I stand in such solidarity (as does my dad) with #MeToo and #ChurchToo and anything that names and addresses toxic masculinity in all its forms. I know, too, that for far too many folks the image of a Father God is one fraught with a complexity of terriblenesses.

At the same time, one of the supposed verities of literature is that the good guy is never as interesting as the bad guy. Literature is replete with awful men who are depicted as awfully amazing: Milton's Satan, Byron's Manfred, Brontë's Heathcliff—and the list goes on. In Marilynne Robinson's work, for example, we've come some way to dispelling that cliché, but without Robinson's skill (or the space of a novel) how can I give adequate testimony to my dad's more than fourscore years?

Admittedly, the bare outline has promise: a child raised in the wildness of 1930s and 1940s Wyoming, a Vietnam veteran, a career Army officer, a witness to the Cold War. Whether working or retired, my dad lived a life of service.

I could tell you of his generosity and thoughtfulness: how he sends me, his unmarried daughter, an anniversary present every year to commemorate my PhD. How he once gave his truck away because he thought a man in his church needed it more.

I could tell you of the ways he prioritized family over career in the choices he made: how he forewent certain advancements to stay with us. Even though he valued and enjoyed his work (and had many professional accolades), there was never any question that he most wanted to be with his family.

I could tell you of his encouragement: how I have so many memories of a childhood where compliments were frequent and affirmation constant. I have never had a single doubt that my father would stand behind me and be proud of me. How he is always ready with "I love you."

I could tell you of his faithfulness and leadership to whatever church he has ever attended: how he gives his time and his resources, but also his commitment. The way he has worked to raise up new generations of leaders, and how he has been intentional to mentor and encourage young ministers.

I could tell you of his wisdom, his patience, his joy at life.

But even as I have searched for just the right words, I know I'm not doing any of this justice. The loveliness we observe in the best people in our lives is never easily conveyed. I suppose the trying is enough—and anyway, my father would always modestly (and no doubt rightly) give all the credit to Christ's sanctifying work in his life.

I often teach a lovely little novel by Elizabeth Gaskell called *Cranford*. The book's main character, Miss Matty, is someone who has lived an unremarkable life in a small English village. But the novel concludes with these lines: "We all love Miss Matty, and I somehow think we are all of us better when she is near us."[19]

I wonder if we could be more intentional about finding the stories of people who have made us better by being near, those folks who consistently plant the "seeds of joy." They have stories worth sharing more broadly. And maybe we could tell them of our appreciation too—and plant some seeds ourselves.

TIPS FOR CULTIVATION

But we shouldn't just plant seeds. Psalm 37:3 instructs us to "Trust in the LORD and do good / Dwell in the land and cultivate faithfulness" (NASB).

For a long time, I wasn't very interested in gardening. I never grew much beyond houseplants, a few self-tending rose bushes, and the occasional tomato. But during a seemingly endless winter of snow upon snow, I fantasized about sunshine and decided to turn a large swath of my backyard (a 25 foot by 25 foot area) into a garden. I began reading seed catalogs and dreaming of summer. Filled with glossy beauty shots of vegetable, fruit, and flower, and a steady incantation of wondrous names like Ruby Queen and Black Krim, Triumph De Farcy and Dragon's Tongue, the imaginative possibilities suggested by these pages were endless—magical beans just waiting to grow into stalks fit for little girls and giants alike to climb.

Of course, tending a garden *is* an imaginative act. To tend a garden is in part to hope—to believe in a harvest yet to come. It is also a commitment to work. Ordering the seeds isn't enough. Planting isn't either.

My first summer of gardening taught me several important lessons about how to cultivate faithfully. Here are a few of them:

1. You must engage the project—there is no such thing as a theoretical gardener.

2. Gardening is an excellent corrective for perfectionism because you control so little of the process.

3. In fact, things sometimes grow in spite of you.

4. Cultivating the soil is very hard work. Rototilling just about killed me. I had to learn to use the machine correctly: not so hard that I was digging holes, not so lightly that I was simply skimming the surface.

5. It's smelly and messy to enrich the soil. But worth it. And completely necessary.

6. Weeds are inevitable. Deal with them when they're small and easy to get rid of. They overrun a garden before you know it.

7. Plants need proper support—a tomato without a cage, a bean without its pole, are unhappy vegetables.

8. Things seldom turn out how you expect—bugs take over, critters invade, or you have a crop of beets beyond your ability to eat them all. Use it as an occasion to laugh, to practice relinquishing control.

9. But some things are predictable, like too much squash or an explosion of cherry tomatoes. Use it as an occasion of generosity.

Because:

1. You're only a caretaker. The soil, the sun, and the rain all come from a greater hand than yours.

The same hand that is, thankfully, tending us too.

I thought about being a caretaker quite a bit when I found myself houseless for a period. I had sold my house in July, but as the closing dragged on and on—we didn't close until the end of September—I had an additional thirty days to move, so well into the semester, I vacated my house of nineteen years.

I should mention a key detail: I hadn't bought replacement accommodations by the time I had to move out at the end of October. Very kind friends, who snowbird in the South part of the year, had offered me the use of their house during my transition. A great relief and a great blessing, to be sure.

But living in someone else's house got me thinking about a theological position I've often heard described: the idea that somehow when we are heaven-focused, we care less about our earthly home. We needn't be especially stewardly because we are, in the words of the old hymn, being "beckon[ed] from Heaven's open door," so we needn't care about the condition of the earthly home that we're only "passing through."[20]

Turns out this sentiment might make a good gospel song, but real life does not bear it out. Certainly, I am aware of the abysmal way people can treat hotel rooms and rental cars. But when folks entrust their beloved house to you, the perspective shifts: you become very, very careful. I didn't want anything stained or scratched, besmirched or broken. It would have been awful to disappoint the magnanimous trust my friends had in me by treating their home in a cavalier way. Or to leave it or its contents dirty and ruined.

I don't need to beat you over the head with the spiritual parallel: the gracious God who entrusts his beloved creation to us. And our only credible response: great, sustained solicitude for all of that creation. But maybe we need to be reminded of the gratitude that should motivate our care for the earth and its inhabitants. I was so deeply touched by my friends' gesture—letting me stay in their house for as long as need be. How could I respond with anything but a spirit of thankfulness and a commitment to increased care for what I had been entrusted with? To do less seemed disrespectful, ungrateful, entitled. Ultimately, home or not, how we take care of wherever we live demonstrates more about our attitude toward the owner than it does about anything else. And by our actions we testify to whether we are grateful guests or self-absorbed squatters, whether we are committed to faithful cultivation or simple exploitation.

"BRITTLE CRAZY GLASS" AND WITNESS-TREES

As much as I like the metaphors of gardening and caretaking, they have limitations, as all metaphors do. Especially because, wrongly developed, they can lead us back to a sense of our own self-sufficiency, our primary importance. So an important addition to our metaphorical collection about the faithful life is through the words of the seventeenth-century poet and clergyman George Herbert and his wonderful poem "The Windows."[21] In this poem, Herbert begins by asking:

> Lord, how can man preach thy eternal word?
> He is a brittle crazy glass;
> Yet in thy temple thou dost him afford
> This glorious and transcendent place,
> To be a window, through thy grace.

I love the image here of Christians as pieces of glass that make up a stained-glass window in a church. God has given us a central role to tell God's story with a kind of fixity over time. But notice this work is at odds with the kind of glass that we are: "brittle crazy glass." Not only are we fragile but "brittle," which, according to the *Oxford English Dictionary*, means "that which breaks faith, inconsistent, fickle." In addition, we are "crazy glass;" that is, glass that is imperfect (we might say "crazed" glass now), or as a seventeenth-century definition would have had it, "damaged or diseased."

Herbert goes on to emphasize our sorry condition as glass. In our natural state, we are "waterish, bleak, and thin." But as the powerful light of God shines through us, it is only then that our colors glow and the story of God comes alive through us:

> But when thou dost anneal in glass thy story,
>   Making thy life to shine within
> The holy preachers, then the light and glory
>   More reverend grows, and more doth win;
>   Which else shows waterish, bleak, and thin.
>
> Doctrine and life, colors and light, in one
>   When they combine and mingle, bring
> A strong regard and awe; but speech alone
>   Doth vanish like a flaring thing,
>   And in the ear, not conscience, ring.

Indeed, in the final stanza, Herbert makes clear that our own words "doth vanish like a flaring thing," with no effect on the "conscience." Instead, it is our embodied faithfulness in a particular place that makes us "holy preachers" because the illumination of the Sun/Son can pour through us and accomplish God's work, bringing the viewer of the stained glass to "strong regard and awe" of the source of that light.

Or maybe we are "witness-trees," what British scholar and naturalist Robert MacFarlane has defined as "originally a tree that stood as a record of property boundaries, marked as such by scores in its bark. Now broadened to mean a tree that has seen remarkable things, that stands as 'a repository for the past.'"[22] Turns out there are many famous "witness-trees" worldwide. Many of the most well-known ones in America are, probably unsurprisingly, at Civil War battlefields, riddled with Union and Confederate bullets. But the one that strikes me the most is the tree on the site of the 1995 Oklahoma City bombing. Now called the Oklahoma City Survivor Tree, this American elm, which stood right next to the Alfred P. Murrah Federal Building, felt the full blast of the explosion, its bark beleaguered with the building's shrapnel of metal and glass, its branches laden with a destroyed car's hood. Officials initially wanted to take down the one-hundred-year-old tree and extract the building's detritus to use as evidence, but community support for the tree as a symbol of survival meant that it now sits as the center-piece of the Oklahoma City National Memorial.

We know from our biology classes how central trees are in pro-ducing the very air we breathe. We've seen the beauty of the bonsai and the sequoia. And it's striking how trees capture the imagination of the biblical writers. The Tree of Life is a star of Genesis and Rev-elation (you can't say that for many other Bible figures besides God). And despite a lack of mobility, trees are not figured as passive. They rather famously "clap their hands" in the Psalms and in Isaiah. They are to provide food for the "foreigner, the fatherless, and the widow" in Deuteronomy (Deut 24:19). And they know their place before God, the source of their flourishing, says Ezekiel 17:24: "All the trees of the forest will know that I the Lord bring down the tall tree and make the low tree grow tall. I dry up the green tree and make the dry tree flourish."

Our culture so often equates rootedness with stodginess, with quiet desperation, with a lack of imagination or ambition. Roaming is much more preferable. People with real ambition, as it goes, leave their hometown as fast as ever they can; no one need stay put in any organization or relationship when change is the highest value. But Psalm 1, one of the very first Bible passages I ever memorized, urges us to be a "person . . . like a tree planted by streams of water / which yields its fruit in its season / and whose leaf does not wither." Notice the attention to being planted, to bearing fruit. To be rooted in God as a witness-tree is a metaphor that might serve to make one well-contented in middle age and beyond when discontent, when "stuckness," when the ennui of place and profession can take over.

Indeed, it is a worthy goal: to be something that lives, even with damage embedded, to testify over a long spell—whatever forest we find ourselves in, whether we are in a dark wood or on the banks of the Jordan.

After all, there is much to testify about: a God who is faithful in big things and small. In Sarah Lindsay's whimsical poem "If God Made Jam,"[23] she imagines how God might engage in a rather ordinary household task and its effects:

If God made jam the jars wouldn't necessarily glow
like Christmas lights or the new home of seventy fireflies,
the berries wouldn't have to be so divine
they dribbled rainbows and healed the sick,
each pip released a *Gloria* when it
cracked between your teeth,
and God's jam would never refuse to touch earthly bread—

Aunt Lydia has worked out this much
since Cousin Bobby told her about a comma
he skipped long ago while learning his catechism.
Now, on a rainy morning, spared the news
that lay in her grass and is too wet to read,
she's flexed her stiff hands and found them able
to slice the bread baked by a friend

and twist the lid from a royal-red jar,
and with the first crusty, raspberry bite
she's ready to affirm God does make jam.
It still counts if people figure among
the instruments that have been put to use,
and Bobby catechized wasn't wrong
when he pictured a deity, willing to work in the kitchen,
who made preserves and redeemed us.

The poem reminds me of Marilynne Robinson's observation that I shared in chapter one: "With all respect to heaven, the scene of miracle is here, among us."[24] As Aunt Lydia understands, God's work does not need to have an extraordinary "glow" to be present—it is everywhere, in all things. In the "earthly" bread and the ordinary raspberries is an alternative vision of the Eucharist as delicious and strength-giving. "God's jam" is definitely there for the needs of earth, even if the bread and jam also spare Aunt Lydia from worrying too much about the now-wet news. The news is less real than the ache in her hands and the provisions of the morning: the essentials. And why? In the clever play on words in the poem's final line comes the affirmation that the God of daily bread is indeed "willing to work in the kitchen," doing the necessary labor ("made preserves") but also continuing alongside us ("made, preserves" as in the original to which this alludes) until our faithfulness is transformed into delicious redemption.

4

Assessing the Hill

I do not wish to treat
friendships daintily,
but with roughest courage.
When they are real, they are not
glass threads or frostwork,
but the solidest thing we know.

RALPH WALDO EMERSON, "FRIENDSHIP"

FOR MANY YEARS I WALKED my dog pretty much every day with one of my closest friends and her dog. In every season. No matter the Michigan weather. Every day we walked through the neighborhood and the little park near my friend's house.

Our motto could have been *solvitur ambulando* ("it is solved by walking") because—no matter the *it*—so it often was for us, even if *solved* more accurately meant "discussed" or "vented about." Still, there is something about the companionableness of walking with another person that allows, perhaps mysteriously, a kind of conversational largesse. Maybe it's the need to find a physical pace that accommodates you both, which signals a commitment to the other's welfare. Maybe it's the lack of other distractions. It's probably those reasons and more. But there *is* a special attentiveness that the best kind of walk seems to make possible.

Lots of folks have written about the spiritual formation of the everyday, or what Kathleen Norris has called "the quotidian mysteries."[1] Though I will not presume to speak for my friend, I will say that for me our daily walk, practiced faithfully through many years, was a holy thing. Holy because it was a part of every day—carved out and set apart. Holy because it was a time of communion with friend and dogs and creation. Holy because it was a time of being Christ to each other—a means of encouragement and a way of carrying each other's needs. How could that not fail to form someone deeply?

Both of the dogs that took those walks have now been gone for more than a couple of years. And my friend has moved away. But often when we talk on the phone, my friend is out walking her current dog, and I can sometimes hear the gravel crunching beneath her feet as she traverses the lake path near her home. She is always apologetic when her commands to the dog punctuate our conversation (as they frequently do).

I never mind. Any way we can take a walk is a holy thing indeed.

It doesn't surprise me, then, that God seems to have walked with his friends too. Some of Jesus' best teaching comes while he is ambling about with the disciples. But the divine predilection for walking starts right in Genesis, when we see God strolling through the Garden of Eden in Genesis 3 and then with Enoch and Noah and Moses. And it's all throughout those first biblical books—as if establishing the importance of God as friend, as companion. Maybe all those verses about the people who "walked with God" are supposed to be read metaphorically, but I like to imagine that someone like Enoch really did literally walk with God. And when he disappeared, it was because his nightly walk with God simply never ended. What a lovely idea.

What if we took seriously the idea that God wanted to be our friend? How would that change our narrative about our relationships with God and with each other? After all, Jesus—criticized for his friendships with tax collectors and sinners, women, and outcasts— centers friendship at the heart of his message, claiming that no love is greater than the sacrificial love for friends (John 15:13). Even by calling us friends, even in figuring his own sacrifice as something for companions (not servants or even siblings), he asks us to follow him into a radical reimagining of relationships: friend of God, friend of each other, friend of creation.

NOT ONLY A "PRIVILEGE FOR PATRIARCHS"

I often teach Alfred, Lord Tennyson's magnificent poem *In Memoriam: A. H. H.* Tennyson began the poem, which he worked on for over fifteen years, after the shockingly premature death at age twenty-two of his best friend, Arthur Henry Hallam. The poem is a meditation on some of the profoundest of the "big questions": theodicy and suffering, faith and doubt, creation and chaos. But in addition, the poem examines the very personal nature of grief—and of love of friend. Each time I bring students to the poem, we discuss Tennyson's struggle to find adequate metaphors for the depth of his friendship. Over and again, he advances different comparisons—parents and siblings, lovers and widows or widowers—to try to make clear what he felt for his lost friend, and over and again, he can only, at best, approximate.

My students agree that the problem isn't only Tennyson's. Even as, generationally, friendship—and not dating—seems to have become ever more valued by young people, friendship just doesn't rate as highly in our language: when we compare "I love you like a sister" to "I love you like a friend," the resulting class laughter tells us everything we need to know about our core beliefs. We still lack a robust way to talk about friendship. And Tennyson's struggle over more than one hundred cantos is reflected in our obituaries, one of the surest registers of what we value as a culture. In the stories of the dead, we observe who gets a final story and why, what gets included (and doesn't), which relationships are selected as essential. Though it is changing perhaps, friendship doesn't feature as much in obituaries—sometimes a really good friend gets a mention, but it's never the default like for families. No matter the actual state of a familial relationship, even estranged family members typically get named. But maybe friends aren't included because, generally, friendship doesn't make the cut in the final accounting of a life. Despite the depths of modern loneliness and studies that chronicle the declining number of close friendships, friendship doesn't count enough in our reckoning of success. Those bonds are beaten out by work and hobbies and memberships. Ironically, everything we tell our college students that vocation *isn't* about ends up being the main things accounted for on the webpages of the local funeral home.

It's why one obituary stood out to me when, in its headline, it singled out the importance of a woman's life as the best friend of a famous person. Intrigued, I read on. Surely, other famous people had best friends—why would this qualify for an obituary in a major newspaper? Surely, that couldn't be important enough? Or so unusual? More research turned up other headlines in other national newspapers that went further, claiming that many people claimed this woman as a friend. Indeed, one article reported she "was known for being the best friend you could find. . . . Everyone who knew her was her friend, and they could always count on her to be welcoming, loyal, nurturing, and kind."[2] The quality of her friendship turned out to be more impressive than her successful work and personal life— also mentioned, but somehow not as important. Testimonies of her talents as a friend were all over social media. The fact that this surprised me—even after all those Tennyson conversations—showed me how deep down these preconceptions lay.

That may be because the message of the church often perpetuates a general American-Christian idolatry of the family. While popular culture, especially TV, has certainly seemed to move (whatever our other critiques may be) toward celebrating a friend-centered ethos—think as far back as *Seinfeld*, *Friends*, and *Sex in the City*—our churches have often continued to behave as if romantic partnership and marriage, and the family unit (that needs must follow) is the highest achievement of a life. And this is true whatever stance on human sexuality one adopts: the couple and family are always the best and the more desirable "achievement." By contrast, when was the last time you heard a sermon exhorting you to be a better friend? Or even telling you what that might look like?

That's a pity because people are so hungry for friendship. The pandemic exposed the loneliness that is at the root of so much of American culture, what Susan Mettes has deemed the "loneliness epidemic."[3] But this was true before Covid-19 struck: a much-cited *Boston Globe* article from 2017 lamented what the headline writer summarized as the "biggest threat facing middle-age men . . . loneliness."[4] We are ever more disconnected, with surveys showing that we have fewer and fewer close friends.

So while the Bible is full of rich metaphors for connection, it is striking how much it has to say about friendship, including God's friendship being extended to us. Certainly, I am not denying the beauty and utility of familial metaphors: God comforting like a mother in Isaiah 66, Jesus as our brother in Hebrews 2, our inclusion as sons and daughters throughout the New Testament. But the Bible is emphatic about both God and Jesus as friend. About the richness of friendships between David and Jonathan; Elijah and Elisha; Daniel and Shadrach, Meshach, and Abednego; between Mary and Elizabeth; between Jesus and John; between Jesus and Martha, Mary, and Lazarus; between Paul and Priscilla and Aquila; and on and on.

There is the worry about seeming irreverent in envisioning God
as "pal," but Scripture doesn't seem so wary: Moses and Abraham,
after all, are both called "friends of God." Moses' conversations with
God were "face to face, as one speaks to a friend" (Ex 33:11). In fact,
in *Whistling in the Dark*, Frederick Buechner observes:

> [Friendship] is not something that God does. It is something
> Abraham and God, or Moses and God, do together. Not even
> God can be a friend all by himself apparently. . . . Is it a priv-
> ilege only for patriarchs? Not as far as Jesus is concerned at
> least. . . . To be his friends . . . we have to be each other's
> friends, conceivably even lay down our lives for each other. It
> is a high price to pay, and Jesus does not pretend otherwise,
> but the implication is that it's worth every cent.[5]

Thus, it is telling that Christ in John 15, the great friendship chapter,
does not use a familial metaphor when he describes the "greatest love"
in the verse I alluded to earlier: "Greater love has no one than this,
that one lay down his life for his friends" (Jn 15:13 NASB). Jesus could,
for example, have easily used "brothers and sisters" in place of
"friends." Such a choice would have been perfectly in keeping with a
metaphor that emphasizes our adoption as children of God. But instead, perhaps drawing on Proverbs 18:24 ("But there is a friend who
sticks closer than a brother"), he says the "greatest love" lies in a different direction. In so doing, Jesus, as usual, asks that we radically
revise our notion of what defines friendship and its requirements.

CASSEROLES AND CAKES AND HONEYGUIDES

A few years ago I had breakfast with one of my former professors,
whose husband had died unexpectedly a few weeks earlier. She had
never been a religious person or very interested in talking about
faith. And yet, when I asked her how she was coping, she answered,
"I think I might join a church."

I tried to not to act surprised as I muttered something vague about it being a good place to consider questions of mortality and eternity.

"No," she said. "It's not that. It's because I've always heard that church people bring casseroles and cakes when there's trouble. And look in on widows. Help them with leaf raking and other chores. I don't have anything like that and it sounds very appealing. Is it true?"

I assured her we were quite expert in the "casseroles and cakes" division and that care of widows was an ongoing imperative throughout the Bible, even if we didn't always do this perfectly. But I was intrigued. It would have been easy to dismiss this as her mistaking church for a social service or a club. Yet it seemed to me that if she were attracted to the church because of seeing a winsome community, that seemed like a positive thing. After all, she knew that the Christians formed the cake-and-casserole brigade, and it was not just a band of random middle-aged women roaming the streets in a hospitality gang. The church she had been observing had been a pretty effective example of living an embodied Christian life. Maybe we dismiss that kind of witness too easily. Maybe we, too, need to be reminded about the testimony of casseroles and cakes, particularly in an era when so many of us are disconnected, lonely, starved for community.

What if extending friendship was one of the principal hallmarks of our witness?

Or perhaps it's not what we bring but what we can assist in finding. Pulitzer Prize–winning science writer Natalie Angier has described how certain indigenous peoples in Africa use birds called "honeyguides" to locate the commodity, rewarding the birds with beeswax.[6] Angier goes on to detail the latest findings showing that there is a specific, well-developed language used between tribespeople and honeyguides—"an extraordinary exchange of sounds and gestures, which are used only for honey hunting and serve to convey enthusiasm, trustworthiness and a commitment to the dangerous business of separating bees from their hives." Indeed, honeyguides actually advertise that they are there to help with a distinct song.

Honey is important in these cultures, according to the article, because it sometimes supplies as much as 80 percent of calories in a month. Interestingly, however, it is not so much collecting the honey that is the problem (though the extremely aggressive bees need very specific handling) as finding it is. Humans understand what to do when they know the honey is there (even if it usually involves at least a few painful stings), but it is much harder for them to find the honey itself.

This lovely little story of symbiosis makes me wonder about the metaphorical honeyguides in our own lives. How might this be a way to talk about the companionship of the Holy Spirit? Who are those folks who signal their willingness to help us find, despite the danger of the besetting bees, the sweet sources of sustenance? To see love and joy and goodness even in the midst of darkness and depression and disappointment. To help us locate the hope of honey rather than live in fear of the bees. How can we become honeyguides ourselves?

BECOMING A BURDEN

That all sounds great, but I think before we go too much further and look at some specific stories of friendship, we need to acknowledge none of this is easy. Even as the Bible tells us that "wounds from a friend can be trusted" (Prov 27:6), it is also full of bad friendships. Psalms 41 and 55, for example, lament the distress that comes from the betrayal by the "familiar friend." The book of Job is an especially painful lesson on how not to grieve with one's friend in loss. And of course, the disciples disappoint over and again until those smaller letdowns culminate in the final betrayals of Judas and Peter (and the others who disperse too) before the crucifixion. It's gut-wrenchingly poignant, isn't it, that in Matthew's account of the moment in the garden after his betrayal is clear, Jesus says to Judas, "Do what you came for, *friend*" (Mt 26:50, emphasis mine). Not that we can say much ourselves: like the disciples, we are imperfect in our relationships too. The rueful old joke that the most miraculous thing about Jesus is that he had twelve good friends as an adult tells us something about our own insecurities and inabilities.

When I was in my thirties, I wrote an article that began tongue-in-cheek:

I've decided to "become a burden." I'm sure my friends will be thrilled to hear it. I realize that I'm already probably a lot for them to bear, but to consciously decide to burden them flies in the face of a lifetime of training. It's pretty difficult to overcome principles that have become more like ingrained rules: always be ready to do more than your share of any work that needs doing, always keep your own personal difficulties in check, and never overstay your welcome. Be competent and be in control. Put another way, as so eloquently stated in *A League of Their Own*, "no crying in baseball."

I come by it naturally. As I was growing up, we were that family in the church that was there for everything: morning and evening Sundays and as many weeknights as were necessary. My mother and father seemed to be president, chair, and leader of every group, committee, and activity. Though I must acknowledge that their service grew out of a real sense of Christian love, they were so ubiquitous that when my mother died unexpectedly, one little girl in my parents' church remarked incredulously to her mother, "But who will make the coffee now that Mrs. Holberg's dead?" Indeed.

In the days following my mother's death, as the innumerable cakes and breads and cookies and pans of lasagna began to pile up on our kitchen counter, I remember wanting to refuse the next kind woman who called to offer us food. After all, *we* did that for *other* people—we were not so helpless as to need it done for us. And when I returned to my job, I certainly had no intention of letting my loss affect my work. I taught my classes, did my work, and kept my emotional business at home.

I know I'm not alone in this struggle against the idolatry of what I heard Barbara Brown Taylor once call "omnicompetence." One time in the staff lunchroom, I ran into one of my campus colleagues who looked pretty frazzled, and so I asked her how she was. After hesitating a moment, she proceeded to tell me about the myriad tasks that were overwhelming her. When she finished, I said I'd pray for her. Her response was telling: "Oh, that's okay—I don't want you to think I'm a bleeding mess or something." No, we certainly wouldn't want anyone to think that. And she's in good company: another woman I know told me that she had refused to let her husband put her on the prayer chain as she was being tested for cancer because, if it wasn't true, think how she "would have put people out." And another colleague, usually the definition of "together," after crying as she told me about a particularly hard week, remarked, "Oh dear, that's the second time you've seen me cry this semester." No, we wouldn't want that either.

But we learn early that being perceived as needy is something to be avoided. In a childhood filled with frequent moves when I would, again, prepare to be the "new girl," my mother would always echo the words of Proverbs 18:24: "To have friends, you have to be friendly," but would also add "Don't expect anyone to extend themselves to you." Now I know she was trying to encourage me to put myself out there—and to manage my expectations about the hard, sometimes disheartening work of breaking into already-established social circles. But in my adulthood, I've wondered if that comment didn't also unintentionally convey the message that I wasn't worthy of the effort. Or only worthy if *I* did enough, if I was suitably low maintenance and didn't put anyone out. Not just that no one *would* extend themselves but that they really didn't *want* to.

Such thinking flies in the face of the friendship of a God who not only pursues us but needs nothing from our side to make us worthy of it. That's hard to wrap your mind around because, despite our real fears to the contrary, being a burden is exactly what we are called to do. Saint Paul worried about being a burden too (see 2 Cor 12:14), even as he wrote to the early churches on more than one occasion, instructing them to "carry each other's burdens" (Gal 6:2). He knew it was essential, but how exactly? And as importantly, how do we work on allowing others to carry our burdens instead of always focusing on how we can carry theirs?

TEARING OFF THE ROOF

As a well-contented "spinster," I have always highly valued my independence, but the flip side is that, like most single people, I have found myself wondering from time to time about what would happen in a crisis. Popular media feeds that fear. And I don't just live alone: my family is dispersed at the corners of America, many, many miles away. So what would happen when I (rather Humpty Dumpty–like) had a very great fall during July of 2016—and in the process, broke several bones in my foot? Six, to be precise, with the whole shebang receiving a fancy French name. (In the words of one of my colleagues, "When an injury gets a name, it's never good.")

And indeed, it was not good at all: no weight-bearing, no driving. Due to the caprices of my surgeon, my surgery date turned into a dance of endless rescheduling—and so I spent August waiting and mostly housebound. When I finally did get to have surgery, I started teaching classes ten days later—still not driving, and getting around campus on a little knee scooter. So passed September, October, and into November as I moved ever so slowly toward walking again. Finally, it was a major achievement when I got to wear shoes on both feet for the first time since July. Hard not to feel like a triumphant toddler!

And maybe that's not too far off since there's nothing like the helplessness that comes with serious injury. All of a sudden there are so many things that you can't do—or things that absolutely require help. Rides arranged, errands carefully planned. Then, too, our medical system—like most of society, to be honest—isn't really set up for people like me who live alone. Instead, the implicit assumption seems to be that everyone has someone at home available to care for them 24-7.

I've always loved the story in Mark 2 where the paralyzed man is healed by Jesus after his friends, who are blocked by the crowd, lower him through the roof of a house. The text says that it took really serious work: "Since they could not get him to Jesus because of the crowd, they made an opening in the roof above Jesus by digging through it and then lowered the mat the man was lying on." We probably usually think about the man who was healed. Or maybe we think about Jesus and his exchange with the man and with the watching Pharisees.

But think about the friends. Imagine caring about your friend's healing so much that you refused to be put off by the crowds. That you wanted to see your friend restored so fiercely that you were willing to literally tear a roof off.

Turns out that's exactly the kind of people who make up my community. Every night in August someone different brought me an amazing meal, each one expressing such tender care for me. In fact, I had a list of people ready to bring meals beyond what I needed. Two friends joked that I was eating too healthily and showed up with trays of hors d'oeuvres, a box full of bakery goodies, and some "adult" slushies, and set up a very happy hour alongside my sofa campsite. Cards and emails and Facebook encouragement were constant. Flowers and plants arrived. A team of folks came and stayed with me in the days after my surgery. Errands were run. My floors were scrubbed and my house was cleaned. Over and again. My laundry was done, and the bed made up with fresh sheets. Over and again. My trash was collected and taken to the curb. Every week. And I was driven to appointments and haircuts and grocery stores and back and forth to wherever I needed going. Every day.

It may be that it is better to give than to receive—but, of course, that's a paradox since without receivers there would be no givers. As I've already noted, I have not been accustomed in my life to be a receiver very often. And yet, my months of incapacity were a powerful—and unexpected—testimony that I am not alone. A stay against anxieties about whether single folks like me will be cared for. An assurance that the kinship of believers really means something quite tangible. And beautifully so. What occurs to me is that "being a burden" presumes a level of vulnerability that most of us don't allow ourselves—unless we are forced. To whom are we willing to reveal ourselves? To whom are we willing to expose the illusion of our own strength? How can we commit to being roof destroyers all?

I'M DREAMING OF A BROWN CHRISTMAS

Maybe part of tearing off the roof is helping each other get to where we need to be. Sometimes when I drive around town, I notice the billboards announcing that Mega Millions or Powerball is currently at some incredible amount in the millions of dollars. Hard to imagine (though I am certainly guilty of such idle speculation) what one would do with all that money. I do know one thing I'd like to do, however, if I ever received such a windfall: I'd hope to imitate the best Christmas gift that I've ever heard of.

It was given by a couple named Michael and Joy Brown. Michael was a writer and performer and Joy a former ballerina who had studied with George Balanchine. They lived with their two young sons in New York City in the 1950s.

They had a dear friend—a fellow artist—who was struggling to make it. Their friend had needed to take a job as an airline reservations clerk and had little time for artistic pursuits. And home was very far away. Despite the joy of spending Christmas with the Browns each year, the holiday was always difficult.

But Christmas 1956 was different. In the branches of their Christmas tree, the Browns placed an envelope for their friend. It read: "You have one year off from your job to write whatever you please. Merry Christmas."

Their friend: Harper Lee.

In the year she was given she produced the first draft of *To Kill a Mockingbird*.

In an article in *McCall's* magazine in December 1961, Lee reflected on the breathtaking quality of her friends' gift. She initially resisted the extravagance of the gesture and raised objections, declaring why it would be impossible for her to accept such a gift. And yet, the Browns were adamant. They believed in her and in her talent: as Lee came to understand, "they wanted to show their faith in me the best way they knew how."

That show of confidence transformed Lee's life, her work, and even her sense of homesickness. The money was nice, of course, but the Browns' love was what was critical:

A full, fair chance for a new life. Not given me by an act of generosity, but by an act of love. *Our faith in you* was really all I had heard them say. I would do my best not to fail them. Snow still fell on the pavement below. Brownstone roofs gradually whitened. Lights in distant skyscrapers shone with yellow symbols of a road's lonely end, and as I stood at the window, looking at the lights and the snow, the ache of an old memory left me forever.[7]

I don't suppose I'll ever be able to give my friend the artist or my friend the poet a year off from their jobs—even though it's one of my primary lottery fantasies, and even though I'm convinced they'd produce amazing works.

I can't go big, but I'm still committed to time as a gift nevertheless—even if it's only in small increments. For instance, for many years my dear friend and I have given each other the Christmas gift of an hour a week. The present of presence. Uninterrupted, intentional conversation for an entire sixty minutes. It may not sound like much, but it is incredibly restorative. I need that time more than I need a sweater or a book or a knickknack.

THE CALCAGNI CLUB

Or maybe it's not only time, but encouragement.

Every time I am in Florence, I spend time meditating on one of my favorite sculptures: the *Pietà* of Michelangelo, often referred to as *The Deposition*. Now housed in the Museo dell'Opera del Duomo, it is one of three depictions of Mary mourning over the body of the crucified Jesus that Michelangelo produced over his lifetime. Unlike the *pietàs* in Rome and Milan, which feature only Mary and Jesus, the Florentine sculpture also includes Mary Magdalene and Nicodemus (or in some interpretations, Joseph of Arimathea). Originally, Michelangelo intended the work for his

Figure 4.1. *The Deposition* by Michelangelo, Museo dell'Opera del Duomo, Florence

own tombstone—and in this deeply personal work, the face of Nicodemus is a self-portrait of Michelangelo himself. In fact, Michelangelo labored over the statue for most of his seventies, but for reasons that are still debated, eight years into the project, he grew dissatisfied with it and tried to destroy it, wielding a hammer that broke off several significant pieces.

I find the piece incredibly evocative, particularly the face of Nicodemus. But a significant part of why I love it is that it is a work that has been repaired. After Michelangelo's attempted destruction, his friend and student Tiberio Calcagni worked to counteract the damage. It was Calcagni who reattached the broken pieces—repairs that can be seen as one looks at the statue. Controversially, he even continued sculpting the face of Mary Magdalene (something of which art historians are, understandably, not big fans). But these things have never really mattered to me: the intensity and beauty of Michelangelo's work is profoundly moving—it's as if it literalizes the brokenness of Christ's body and heightens the sorrow of Mary, Mary Magdalene, and Nicodemus.

Whenever I teach British literature of the early nineteenth century, the time of the Romantics, we examine poems like Percy Shelley's "Ozymandias" and John Keats's "Ode on a Grecian Urn" that make quite persuasive arguments for the power of the poet, of the creator, of the original mind. It may be obvious, given the subject of this book, that I don't disagree. But I want to make sure we think, too, about the limitations of only looking to the solitary genius; it seems like a rather limited way to think about the creative process. What of the other necessary roles? Call it the Calcagni Club, but I believe there is a need in the world for the appreciator, the bolsterer, the friend of the artist, whose primary gift is not creative but supportive. When I teach, I love to tell the stories of all the times we would not have incredible literature without the sometime interventions, the sometime encouragement of people brave enough to believe in the talents of their friends. Here are a few of the people on my gratitude list:

- Nicholas Ferrar, who was entrusted by George Herbert with the manuscript of *The Temple*. As Herbert was dying, he told Ferrar he should either burn the manuscript or, if he felt it had any merit, publish it. Imagine a world without Herbert's work.

- Robert Bridges, who was a poet laureate himself, but who cheered on his friend Gerard Manley Hopkins throughout his life and worked after Hopkins's death to bring out the first edition of his poetry. Today Hopkins is the far more esteemed poet, yet I bless the memory of Bridges and his role in promoting his friend.

- Max Brod, who refused to destroy the work of Franz Kafka as Kafka had directed him to in his will.

And then there's Johanna Bonger. Married to Theo van Gogh, she spent most of her adult life promoting her brother-in-law, Vincent. A long-form piece in the *New York Times Magazine* chronicled how she is "the force who opened the world's eyes to his genius."[8] It was amazing to read of the effort it took on her part, a lifetime of dedicated advocacy.

One wonders what art and literature languishes or never emerges because it lacks a Calcagni, a Ferrar, a Bonger. Yet the Romantic myth of the solitary genius continues to have a strong hold on our imaginations—even though it is not only a myth, but a toxic one at that because most creatives know just how much bucking up they need. It's why the acknowledgments section is so fun to read; in it we get insight into the circles of family and colleagues and friends that enable imagination to flower and flourish. It's why I love book groups and craft fairs and student art ventures and amateur musical performances: all places to cultivate our inner Barnabas by encouraging, even if only by our attendance, the talents of others.

But it's not just writers and artists—it's saints too. The first time I visited the beautiful town of Assisi, home of Saint Francis, I took a tour of the spectacularly frescoed Basilica of San Francesco d'Assisi led by one of the Franciscan brothers. It's an awesomely (in the true sense of that word) impressive place—a testament to the incredible (and continuing) impact of Francis's example on generations of Christians. Still, one of the things that struck me most came when we visited the room that held some of Francis's few belongings, saved by his disciples—among them a cloak and, surprisingly for the barefooted Francis, shoes. These all, our brother told us, were gifts from the Lady Jacoba. And then he told us her story.

A Roman noblewoman, Jacoba de Settesoli married into the Frangipani family but was widowed young. When Francis came to Rome to seek permission for his order from the pope, Jacoba went to hear him preach and then invited him to her house to seek his advice about how she could live a devoted religious life. But Francis urged her to remain outside the cloister, and some traditions have it that he established the Third Order Lay Franciscans for her. She turned over her business affairs (and substantial landholdings) to her sons and devoted her life to charity, providing, for example, substantial financial backing to Franciscan works.

She also became Francis's close friend. And here's where the shoes and the cloak come in: so close a friend that she was the only one who could (or would) convince Francis as he grew sicker in his last days to take better care of himself and put on some shoes, already.

She's also the person he wanted with him as he was dying. He sent for her, but as legend has it, she was already at the gates, bringing with her the delicious almond cookies she was known for—and which he especially liked.

When she arrived in Assisi, Francis's disciples—in the manner seemingly common to all disciples—didn't want to let her in, in this case because she was a woman, forbidden to enter the monastery. But Francis wouldn't hear of it and demanded that "Brother Jacoba" should be welcomed. She remained with him until he died. And when she died she was buried in the basilica's crypt, near Francis. To this day, Franciscans exchange almond cookies on the date of Francis's death, acknowledging her sweet role in his life.

In the great splendor of that basilica and the grand narrative of Francis's life that it presents, I was deeply moved that the brother took time to tell us this smaller story. Awed by their goodness and their seeming strength, we sometimes forget that saints need taking care of too, and that the work of providing sturdy shoes and favorite cookies and deep friendship is equally God's work. Thanks be to God for the Lady Jacobas of the world and what they make possible in the lives of the saints—that is, in our lives. And for the comfort that comes from friends who show up, even before we know we need them.

FOR JRB

Her picture hangs on the wall of my office as she was as a young WAVE cryptographer during World War II. In profile, her upturned face shows a woman brimming with self-confidence and joie de vivre, bright and striking and determined. Though she has been gone now for over a decade, our many-year friendship—despite the large gap in our ages—was deeply formative in making me the kind of friend I continue to strive to be. We met on a church committee, and as she grew more homebound, I began to visit her each week. Intellectually and spiritually, she sparkled. Or perhaps a better word is *sparked*. Whenever we talked and my own thinking was sharpened by hers, Proverbs 27:17, "As iron sharpens iron, so one person sharpens another" came to mind. During my weekly visits, even as she was undergoing excruciating rounds of chemotherapy, we spoke of politics and presidents from Roosevelt to Bush; of the controversies racking the denomination to which we both belong; of books and family and mutual acquaintances. On all these topics she had a sharp eye and an even sharper tongue. Once we were discussing a sermon in which the minister had asserted that he had always imagined the great cloud of witnesses described in Hebrews as like a stadium crowd at a race, cheering us on. I asked her if she really believed that people looked down on us from heaven, and she replied she didn't think so. "After all," she said, "heaven is supposed to be a place without pain and suffering and looking down on us probably wouldn't give them much peace." I thought that sounded about right.

Lest I drift too far into praise—something she would have undoubtedly called me on—I admit she was impatient with nonsense, opinionated, honest about her struggles with hyper-competence and the attendant difficulty of receiving. Our similarities made friendship easy. Although I did not know it at first, she had a cancer that grew from manageable to unmanageable—and grappling with the inevitability of her death was very difficult. I should have been prepared. It's not as if I have never experienced the death of someone close to me before. A childhood minister, the father of my best friend in late elementary and early junior high, died in a plane crash when I was in high school. My grandparents are all long-departed. My mother's premature death. I've had to do some thinking on "the resurrection of the body" when we recite the Apostles' Creed in church.

But somehow a friend is different. Or perhaps it felt different because this was the first time I had known a close friend in this situation. Nevertheless, she went a long way in preparing me. When we went to lunch to celebrate the completion of her chemotherapy, I was my usual Tiggerish self, enthusiastically cheerful about her return to better health. When I told her how pleased I was that she was better, she looked me square in the eye and said, "But you know I know it's only temporary."

I froze, hoping not to cry in the restaurant, before finally stammering, "Well, isn't everything?"

"Yes," she responded, "but it's the attitude toward the temporariness that's important. Too many people spend all their time worrying about how long they have left, so they don't end up enjoying any of the time they do have. I intend to enjoy it."

That hit home because I know my own impulse is exactly the opposite: I want to solve every problem and make everything better. My friends tease me about one of my most-repeated mantras: "I won't let that beat me." But that's not ever the job of friendship. I read of a study in which a group of students was given heavy backpacks and taken to the bottom of a very steep hill.[9] There the students stood either alone or with friends. Asked to assess the incline of the hill, they measured the severity of the ascent in front of them quite differently: those with friends thought the hill was much less steep than those who stood alone. What's more, the hill seemed the least steep to the groups of students who had been friends the longest. The lesson seems clear: that in the name of the one who called us friend, we help each other face the arduous climb that lies before us.

Dame Felicitas Corrigan of Stanbrook Abbey was a noted nun with considerable achievements, but when I read about her and her many outstanding contributions, it was the following assertion that stayed with me long after I finished reading: "Her greatest genius was reserved for friendship."[10] I can think of no lovelier epitaph. Corrigan's motto, "*Porta patet, cor magis* (the door is open, more so the heart)," suggests a largesse of spirit that we would do well to imitate as we seek to open ourselves to those people who will in turn act as our support, propping us up when necessary. When we over-worry about equity, about who has done what for whom and if what we have done back is enough or too much or nowhere near enough, we make the business of friendship into a commercial transaction. And friendship is no place for such economics—or strict recordkeeping. The thirteenth chapter of 1 Corinthians tells us that love keeps no record of wrongs, but love shouldn't keep a record of rights either. I like Emily Dickinson's formulation in a letter to Samuel Bowles in 1858, "My friends are my estate."[11] I love the idea that it is the people who have invested in us (and we in them) that form our true wealth—a condition full of fortune indeed.

But how we carry them—and equally how we allow ourselves to be carried by them—in prayer and in the thousand mundane and not so mundane ways we find to encourage them attests finally to how strong our conviction is that, with the writer of Psalm 68, it is ultimately God "who daily bears our burdens" (Ps 68:19).

Each week until my friend died, we talked and laughed and drank iced tea. When she was able to come to church, I worshiped with her and her husband. And every week, we wished each other God's peace—for surely that is all we can hope for now and hereafter.

5

A Witness
Ready to Serve

I scrub the long floorboards
in the kitchen, repeating
the motions of other women
Who have lived in this house.
And when I find a long gray hair
floating in the pail,
I feel my life added to theirs.

JANE KENYON, "FINDING A LONG GRAY HAIR"

WHAT IF WE HAVE GOTTEN the story of Martha of Bethany all wrong?

How often is Martha held up as being exactly the wrong kind of person—well, let's be honest, the wrong kind of woman. Too bossy, too taken up with the immediate demands of her day. She's let her job as hostess frazzle her away from the holy. And it's not just Martha—it's the chastisement of active women like her. After all, the "right" kind of Christian woman sits quietly at Jesus' feet, a model, as the popular 2000 book declared, of *How to Have a Mary Heart in a Martha World*. Having a Martha heart seems out of the question.

We've spent the last several chapters thinking through the ways in which story might make us more capacious in our accounting for God and for ourselves by helping us be attentive to the constructs and conventions of narrative. What if earlier readings of the Martha story are limited, in part, because we haven't recognized the genre in which it partakes? What I mean by "genre" is a kind of story that can be recognized because of certain shared characteristics. Most of us, for example, can easily spot a mystery or a Western or a romance because we've seen the same elements before in similar stories or films—the British country house, the stranger come to town, the meet-cute.

What if instead we thought of Martha's account in Luke 10 not as a dismissal of her work, but instead as a story of vocation: that hers is in the same genre as that of Peter being called away from his fishing or Matthew being called away from tax collecting. Luke 10, then, is about Martha's call to discipleship—the "one thing needful" (Lk 10:42 KJV). Jesus is not dismissing Martha's labor, but rather he is making the radical claim that it isn't her inherent job as a woman or her highest job as a person. She is not a second-class citizen, debarred from learning and sitting under the tutelage of a rabbi, like her culture tells her she is—she can be a full participant in his ministry and is being invited to sit with his teaching. In other words, he is telling her that her learning from him is more important than her traditional role of serving him supper! What a surprising statement. The role Martha has been taught to believe she has to fulfill to be worthy (and by extension, other women like her sister) is obliterated by Jesus' praise of Mary, who is already pursuing the freedom of not being boxed in by "shoulds."

And I'd argue we've massively misread Mary too. Instead of a quiet, passive woman, Mary quite unexpectedly has left the kitchen and already claimed her discipleship by joining the men. Mary, then, is quite active in her rejection of gendered expectations (as we see later when she again breaks the rules by anointing Jesus with costly perfume in John 12—a role previously reserved only for men). No woman had ever anointed a king before. When Martha complains to Jesus that Mary needs to help her, she is really asking Jesus to confirm where Mary's "place" is. But Jesus does no such thing. Instead, outspoken Martha needs to hear her own call out of the kitchen, needs Jesus to reassure her where her most important work and identity lies.

And like the male disciples and their stories of being called away from their initial jobs, Martha has an interaction with Jesus that asks her to see her original work within the deeper calling of Christ. Like Peter who now fishes "for people" (Mt 4:19), Martha has her work redefined by Jesus. It should not surprise us that Martha's story shares Luke 10 with the parable of the Good Samaritan. That parable is also all about upending genre expectations, where character after character behaves differently than how they are supposed to. And, as importantly, it insists that hospitality lies in presence, not perfection.

With this genre-focused lens, we know that Martha's story is a vocational one because when we next encounter her interacting with Jesus (right before the raising of Lazarus), she engages him in an intellectual and theological discussion as any good disciple would have had with their rabbi. Her relationship with Jesus is both honest and loving (in fact, the text asserts Jesus' love for her first) and through it, she provides a model of discipleship that shows someone who is able to assert Christ's divinity, even as she interrogates him sharply. She does not hold back in her questions or her critiques (including reminding Jesus of Lazarus's smelly condition after four days in the tomb), and he welcomes her as she is. Notice that he does not tell her about the "one thing needful" now because she has chosen it by racing out to engage with him. He addresses her as his disciple, speaking to her some of the profoundest lines in Scripture: "I am the resurrection and the life" (Jn 11:25-26).

Confident of her primary role as a disciple, she also seems settled in her secondary work, such that in our final glimpse of her in John 12, it is simply reported, "Martha served" (Jn 12:2). Importantly, too, she does not join in scolding Mary for her lavish bestowal of the expensive nard on Jesus. That makes sense to me—as do the Apocryphal stories that tell of her subduing dragons and spreading the gospel in the post-resurrection era. That sounds about right too.

Reclaiming Martha's story as analogous to the call of other disciples gives us another way of thinking about narratives of vocation—important for the way we think about our own callings, for the way we define success. If you've been around Christian higher education, you'll know *vocation* has become one of the biggest buzzwords of the last twenty years. At my university, we talk a good deal about it. It's a big part of our first-year programming. It's one of four all-university goals in our "educational framework"—a document that explores "the enduring characteristics or qualities of thinking, doing, and being that mark a Calvin graduate."[1] And it's one of the required components of the senior capstone class students must take in their majors, a class I teach almost every fall. Still, I've wondered if we're telling the right stories about calling, if we're highlighting the right models. Students often grow weary of all the vocation chatter and sometimes seem to default to a vision of calling that is less robust than we would hope, especially after four years of effort with them. The way we interpret stories like Martha's is important because it reveals what our faith communities believe are our narrative possibilities. That is, if we are people of faith, the stories available to us are shaped by how we read the models presented to us in Scripture. Of course, these are often highly contested and culturally situated. How can we narrate a compelling and theologically sophisticated notion of vocation?

BOTH SIDES NOW

It wasn't until my thirties that I even considered not wearing a slip. This is not, perhaps, the most shocking admission, either because it strikes you as silly or TMI or maybe because you are young enough to have no idea what such a garment is. But such small but important life markers are telling. And it's related in part to why reenvisioning Martha's story is so important to me.

When I watched Hulu's recent miniseries *Mrs. America*—the story of the drive to ratify the Equal Rights Amendment, chronicling both "women's libbers" and the ERA's opponents, most notably Phyllis Schlafly—it was like watching my childhood on the screen.[2] Though both sides represented have criticized the show, the series was not only grounded in historical sources, but, as with the best of creative nonfiction, it also felt right. Part of that is down to the incredible costumes and set design. The interiors take me right back to my seventies childhood. In one episode, for example, one of the anti-ERA women uses the exact Tupperware container (down to the color) I inherited from my mother. Part is the portrayal of these women as quite human and very flawed. It doesn't paper over the differences among feminist leaders, nor does it downplay the ambition and drive of Schlafly and her allies. The series is unapologetic that these women were "difficult" (whatever your definition of that might be) and that they deployed power in ways that our culture is still not completely comfortable with.

As a member of Gen X, these are the women I grew up with. Both sides.

At school, girls like me were told we could pursue anything we liked. Sports opened to us because of Title IX. We witnessed the firsts of Sally Ride and Sandra Day O'Connor and Margaret Thatcher. We sang songs from *Free to Be, You and Me* (also featured in *Mrs. America*) with its critique of housework and gender roles.[3]

My parents encouraged me into every activity, celebrated every academic achievement, never pressured me to conform or dumb myself down. Although the films of the eighties show just how pervasive sexism was in my high school days, the message I received was that women could and should achieve. Dressed in our culottes and jeans, we were supposed to be the fulfillment of second-wave feminism's hopes. We would be the first women able to "have it all."

But if you were a church girl, particularly in a more traditional denomination, the message was oh, so different. In my upbringing, I never once heard a woman preach or knew any ordained women. People in favor of ordained women, I heard, "did not have a high view of Scripture." I never met a woman elder, though when my grandmother became a deaconess, I was incredibly proud (though at the time I couldn't have articulated why). There were women speakers: at women's events or, in church, if they were missionaries or "sharing" (not preaching and not talking from the pulpit). And they could teach Sunday school and Vacation Bible School. Or, as in *Mrs. America*, they could lead women's groups. In Christian determinations of "ladylike" and "feminine," slips and pantyhose and girdles and dresses were very much required, much as they are for the impeccably coiffed women in *Mrs. America*. I never wore pants to church, not even to the freezing-cold outdoor Easter "sunrise service" my family attended every year. When I asserted my admiration for the judge Deborah in high school Sunday school, I was told that she wouldn't have been a leader except that a man had "shirked his duty" (see Judg 4–5). When I left for graduate school in 1990, another woman in my church asked me if I wouldn't rather have an MRS. than a PhD.

I make no claim here that my experience is unique or surprising: my story is shared by so many women in my generation. Ada Calhoun's *Why We Can't Sleep* synthesizes the experience of Gen X women and the ways that the experiences and expectations of our youth have often led to crisis in midlife, and numerous scholars and writers have recorded the fraught history of the church and the stories it has allowed about gendered participation. And yet being a woman raised in such a transitional time is a story that needs chronicling by as many people as possible. I know this because I often teach a course in gender and literature, and I have long found that students usually have little idea of the histories of those that came before them. So I ask my students to interview their mothers and grandmothers, fathers and grandfathers, aunts and uncles— and other people older than they are—to understand more of other generations' experiences, lest they be lost or taken for granted. In hearing these stories, I hope their sense of history will be deepened and their sense of their own possibilities expanded. After all, it's never too late to hear and live into new versions of stories.

After many years when I declined nominations, I finally accepted a call to serve as an elder in my church just a couple of years ago. In some ways, this should be no big deal. While I was in graduate school, I intently studied the role of women in the church, reading as widely and deeply as I could in theological works. My minister at the time, the Reverend Earl Palmer, also taught on the topic, modeling how one could be faithful to Scripture. All of which helped me come to the conclusion that a person could hold to the ordination and full participation of women in leadership. I came to know and admire and to learn from many gifted women pastors. So my own participation as an elder has long been a possibility for me, at least intellectually.

I found actually proceeding through the nomination process, however, extremely moving. In ways, to be honest, that I found quite unexpectedly surprising. The sheer mundaneness of it, for one thing. Watching *Mrs. America* and remembering all the tumult around gender roles in my upbringing (which continues for others in various branches of contemporary American Christianity), I would have never imagined as a child that I would be nominated to be an elder in middle age and that the nomination would seem like a matter of course. There was no kerfuffle nor any suggestion of second-class citizenship (a.k.a. you can only do it because some man shirked his duty). Just a loving invitation to use my gifts alongside everyone in my church. With the assumption that men and women are both given authority to make decisions together for the good of the kingdom. And all of this rooted in Jesus' clear call to women to find their identity as disciples first—and confirmed when the risen Savior shows himself first to a woman and empowers her to proclaim that amazing news. That is the work for women (and men) of every generation, whatever our histories and circumstances. No slip required.

SIGNIFICANT SOIL

Once we have clarity about to whom God's call extends, we can consider the nature of the work to which we are being called. We know that work is important to God; after all, the Bible begins and sets a pattern of describing God's work with God's role as a universe-builder. God as worker is everywhere: the gorgeous Psalm 104, for example, chronicles a God for whom working mightily—in a range of metaphorical professions—is a central aspect of God's identity. And central for God's people as well (see verse 23). Indeed, even before the fall, people were given jobs to do of naming and stewarding. So what, then, are some of the characteristics of worthy work?

When I was ordained as an elder, it seemed joyfully providential to me that it was on the day celebrated in the Roman Catholic tradition as Martha's feast day. As this chapter has already made clear, it has always felt like her story helps to make my own possible. This joining into a larger story, too, puts me in mind of the poem that opens this chapter, where Jane Kenyon describes scrubbing the kitchen floor.

Her labor is not only her own—instead, as she scrubs and then "find[s] a long gray hair, floating in the pail," she reflects on the women who had done this task before her and declares, "I feel my life added to theirs."[4] This notion is a critical corrective to the vocation we so often hear encouraged: something fundamentally individualistic, based in personal passion above all. As it goes, our work is supposed to be central to our identity and to our self-satisfaction. It is thought to be essential that you are "doing what you love," no matter the cost. Annie Dillard's famous essay, "Living Like Weasels," for example, imagines us emulating the weasel in its intense commitment:

> The thing is to stalk your calling in a certain skilled and supple way, to locate the most tender and live spot and plug into that pulse . . . a weasel lives as he's meant to, yielding at every moment to the perfect freedom of single necessity. I think it would be well, and proper, and obedient, and pure, to grasp your one necessity and not let it go, to dangle from it limp wherever it takes you. Then even death, where you're going no matter how you live, cannot you part. Seize it and let it seize you up aloft even, till your eyes burn out and drop; let your musky flesh fall off in shreds, and let your very bones unhinge and scatter, loosened over fields, over fields and woods, lightly, thoughtless, from any height at all, from as high as eagles.[5]

Dillard's "single necessity" seems a long way from the "one thing needful." As romantically "go for the gusto" and carpe diem–y as the actions of Dillard's weasel—with its burned-out eyes and un-hinging bones—sound, her description seems quite at odds with Kenyon's depiction of floor-scrubbing: repetitive, unglamorous, generation-connecting. And not based in the intensity of a single call. Kenyon's Martha-work, as we might call it, is not necessarily rooted in keen personal desire or fulfillment, but in a sense of what needs to be done as service. This seems true not just in domestic contexts but in professional contexts as well. When I think about my own work life as a professor, about the very work of teaching itself, I know that despite pedagogical innovations and technological advances, some things never change. In fact, it feels like much of what runs the classroom is housekeeping: prepping and grading and writing and recording various things. Over and over and over. And like chores like laundry or vacuuming or cleaning bathrooms, just as one round is done, another round seems to need to begin. Then one adds the cycle of department meetings and report writing and and and . . .

Now, I don't actually mind chores too much, but sometimes they feel more chore-y, more wearisome, than at others. But then I go to events like our year-end faculty tribute dinner, and I witness again all the work my colleagues are doing across campus. I hear the success stories of their scholarship, their amazing community engagement, their immense time invested in students in and out of the classroom. I see a retiring colleague—one who spent countless hours on thankless college-wide projects in addition to teaching and research and all the rest. And I feel again the worthiness of the work, the holiness of the quotidian, the necessity of the daily drudge.

I'm reassured by what T. S. Eliot observes in the *Four Quartets*: that the mark of success, the way to find contentment, is to "nourish . . . the life of significant soil."[6] In other words, cultivating a life characterized by aiming to be really good metaphorical dirt. Working to make the ecosystem of one's life a richer, more vibrant environment. This isn't a grand or fancy aspiration—but it is absolutely vital: Am I contributing to a climate where things will grow and thrive? Or am I—through overcommitment and stress, bitterness or anger—making it less fertile? Am I helping things grow in my own life and in others? That is, is my presence adding nutrients or leaching them away? And ultimately, since I'm going to end up as actual dirt eventually, has my work left rich hummus for the generations that follow me, so that things continue to grow? Dirt isn't solitary or heroic. It's communal and humble. As Kenyon perceives, our vocation is not accomplished in isolation. Though I would wager that we tend to think of the word *colleague* as a reference to something we *are* rather than something we *do*, I am quite struck that the *Oxford English Dictionary* shows that the word *colleague* is not just a noun—it's a verb.

> colleague, v. [Old French *colliguer, colleguer,* to join in alliance, unite, < Latin *colligare* to bind together]
>
> 1. to join in alliance, to ally, unite, associate.
>
> 2. to enter into a league or alliance; to unite; to cooperate for a common end; also in a bad sense, to conspire, cabal.[7]

Notice here that the definition focuses not on our individual accomplishments, but on the action of our common work. Of course, the definition also names our tendency to misbehave (the temptation to become a clique or a club) as much as it describes the possibilities of collaboration. A good warning. But vocation, then, might be better thought of not so much as a call to individual career but as the voice of God calling us to join the long line of laborers who did not grow "weary in well doing" (Gal 6:9 KJV).

Here's one picture of what that might look like: many years ago I was on vacation visiting my sister and her family in the Pacific Northwest. While there, I spent the day with my then seven-year-old niece, Sally, and her first-grade class on their field trip to the beach. The class had been preparing for the visit by learning all about the aquatic creatures that could be found along the shore. The kids had a long list of flora and fauna they were supposed to be able to identify: jellyfish, sea stars (known in my day as starfish), sea cucumbers, eels, crabs and clams, sea anemones, sea lettuce and kelp, limpets, and barnacle-crusted rocks. When we arrived, the naturalist on duty instructed all of us on how to successfully navigate the beach, giving particular emphasis on how to interact with the environment as we were searching. The rules struck me as something like a Mary Oliver poem:

Be careful where you walk.

Don't poke at any living creature you find, but approach it gently.

Pay attention.

Fully briefed, the kids were put in teams, given a magnifying glass and a sheet of animals and plants to find, and set loose to go and find them. Wild enthusiasm followed. Witnessing the exuberance of it all was simply delightful. I mean, what joy in finding a barnacle! The wonder of an entire field of starfish! The amazement of yet another crab! And then another. And another! I was rather surprised that it all never seemed to grow old: for the whole morning the kids excitedly raced from one tidal pool to the next, from the shore to the beach—and after lunch, more of the same. Their capacity for completely engaging creation was inspiring and perhaps a tad convicting. Three crabs and a starfish in, I was ready for a Starbucks. For me the day was repetitive and wet and awfully sandy—and yet, the joy of searching (and finding) together never left the children. That seems like something we could all emulate in the drudgery that makes up so much of "adulting."

ON NOT BECOMING A CABBAGE PLANTER

Conversations about vocation are often insufficient or frustrating because they imply that if one makes the right choices, all shall be well. I've noticed in some meetings I've been in of late that "mapping" seems to be one of the metaphors of the moment. As in, "We need to map this course content onto these student learning objectives," or as a replacement for introducing a discipline as in Gerald Rau's

Mapping the Origins Debate.[8] Academic jargon aside, I wonder about mapping in the future tense, as it were. Can things be mapped that are being traveled toward? Don't we have to travel and make the map as we go or alternately, arrive and then look back to make a map? Does the notion of mapping imply a hope that greater clarity of direction is possible? A sense of control that comes with turn-by-turn directions? Maybe. I get what people are attempting with this language—and of course, I'm not saying there's any harm in "plotting a course" (though that strikes me as quite different from mapmaking since the former relies on a map already made). But it made me wonder what we buy into when mapping becomes a dominant metaphor. Whenever I teach my eighteenth-century British literature course, I include Laurence Sterne's highly inventive novel *The Life and Opinions of Tristram Shandy.* Sometimes thought of as a postmodern novel before there was postmodernism, it is a book full of digressions and meta-commentary as it examines the very nature of constructing a life in fiction (or really any biography, for that matter). To give you a sense of Sterne's project: it is so digressive that it takes the narrator over four volumes of the book to even be born.

Or is it really digressive after all? One of the big questions of the novel is what constitutes "the life"? Where does it begin? What narrative elements get to be included? How much context is needed? Was Aristotle really right in his *Poetics* about the clear direction of plot when he advanced that "beginning, middle, and end" notion?

The novel's answer acts as a critique of the assumption of textual—and therefore biographical—linearity. Instead, Sterne's novel argues strongly that our story is not a simple recitation of facts that move smoothly from point to point to point. Instead, asserting that only "cabbage planters" care about straight lines, Tristram literally illustrates the ridiculousness of traditional notions of biography by claiming that the novel's first four volumes resemble the following:

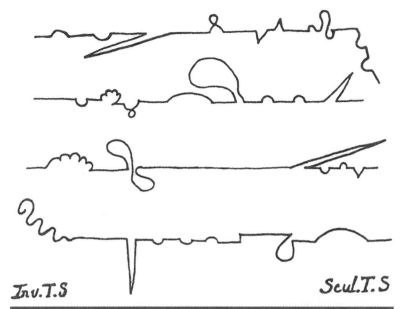

Inv.T.S   *Scul.T.S*

Figure 5.1. The Plot Lines of Laurence Sterne's *Life and Opinions of Tristram Shandy, Gentleman*, from the first edition

These crazy lines are supposed to be amusing—critiquing those who think they can make visual sense of the twists and turns of Tristram's discursive plotting. But in another way they should also be comforting. Even if they could somehow capture the plot (debatable), they would tell us something important about the shape of a life—that it definitely does not go in a straight, predictable, and most importantly, controllable line. It's not the story we often offer as normative, though: I encounter too many folks who worry that their lives are not unfolding as they should because they are not making "forward progress," who have heard too many stories that erase the messy journey and just show the finished map. Too many folks who dismiss the day, the season, as digression—when it's really simply a turn in the road.

And really: Why are we so committed to having a map? As David Wagoner's poem "Lost" suggests, "Wherever you are is called Here," and we're never really lost, especially if we pay attention to the creation that surrounds us.[9] You are here—and that is the here that matters. This is the place where the work needs doing now.

YOUR OWN KIND OF MUSIC

But lovely as all the preceding sounds, we know that dominant cultural narratives push against an embrace of Eliot's "significant soil" and Sterne's messy mapping. Years after I first watched it, I still think often of the Oscar winner for Best Documentary Feature in 2013, *20 Feet from Stardom*, a fascinating examination of the lives and careers of several backup singers—immensely talented women with incredible voices.[10] But there's a tension: while the film wants to celebrate the undeniable talents of these women, it also seems to want us to lament that they "didn't make it."

And it's true: one wonders at the vagaries of gender, race, connections, timing—and sheer chance—that seemed to work against these women being more widely known. Why did stardom elude them? Especially when their talent is so incontrovertible. It doesn't seem fair.

But I wonder if the film is asking the wrong questions. Its philosophy (I might even say its theology) is clear: one job is more significant (because it gets more recognition) than the others. Are we saying that those who work in the background are somehow less valuable because the spotlight doesn't shine on them? That singing lead is more worthy than singing together or in support? At one point in the film, Stevie Wonder humorously demonstrates how his music simply wouldn't work without the singers who surround him—it would just be a series of random "uhhs" and "ahhs," not the rich call-and-response they all achieve together. Songs don't actually work unless all the voices are there. And yet, the film's point seems to posit a version of the disgruntled foot in 1 Corinthians 12—which doesn't feel valued because it's not a hand (1 Cor 12:15). That's not the Christian ideal of vocation, even as it's a very tempting one.

And what is "making it," anyway? The film implies that because (with one notable exception) none of the women had long solo careers, that because none of them had achieved household-name status, there was something sad in what they have done. So fame is the standard of a life well-lived?

One woman in the film complicated the narrative, however— and she emerged for me as the most inspiring person in the film. It is indisputable that Lisa Fischer has an incredible voice. She has sung with pretty much anyone you can name. She has won a Grammy. She tours with the Rolling Stones—and has on every tour since 1989.

More importantly, though, of all the women profiled in the film, she was gracious and clearly at ease with herself. She didn't seem to have internalized that she was less talented (or less of a person) because she wasn't the headliner. She seemed full of joy. And clearly loved to sing any time she got the chance. Didn't matter where or with whom. In representing a very different orientation toward success, her story made the entire film worthwhile because she didn't invite pity at not making it in some system that only valued stars. At the film's end, one admires the talent of all the other singers, but it is Fischer's life that is the triumph.

What counts as success is only part of the problem, however. Another narrative that infects the church as deeply as anywhere else is the one that valorizes busy-ness and overwork as marks of the highest achievement. Every industry has a version of this, but academia's take is the one I live within. In 2018, for example, "Academic Twitter" went a little crazy when Jay Van Bavel of NYU first reposted and commented on an *Inside Higher Ed* piece that had reported that, according to one study, faculty at Boise State University averaged over sixty hours a week at work.[11] But the online party really got hopping when Yale sociologist Nicholas Christakis chimed in on Twitter, claiming "I tell my graduate students and post-docs that if they're working 60 hours per week, they're working less than the full professors, and less than their peers."[12] Fireworks ensued. Though Christakis became more nuanced as he answered many of the hundreds of comments that followed, this debate about workload highlighted many of the deepest divides and insecurities in academia.

My own institution has experimented with a faculty workload study to try and assess how faculty are spending their time and to find ways to make sure our work is appropriately distributed and compensated. While I appreciate the effort to recognize inequity, I'm not sure these kinds of studies work all that well. When it came to my own self-reporting (and I did my best—I really did), I realized later how much underreporting I had done. I decided not to worry: to be honest, if I had reported how much I actually worked, I'm afraid even now that somewhere a "life-work balance" crisis team would be preparing for some kind of intervention.

Now you may think that this is the point in the chapter that I turn to something about cultivating healthy equilibrium or practicing better sabbath or some such. That's very important—and I do think more of our vocation talk should center on giving permission for rest and the like. But that's not where I'm going. Instead, it turns out it doesn't bother me that I'm not going to get every jot and tittle accounted for in the official reckoning of faculty work. And it also doesn't bother me to have had to record numerical evidence of just how much time I do spend on work. I love what I do—Kuyperianly, every square inch—and I feel lucky to get to do it. What's more, when the survey asked a version of "What can be done to make things more equal?" my response was, not much. Here's why.

I used to not be so magnanimous. It used to irritate me when people would tell me how extraordinarily busy they were when I knew that—objectively—they were not. High-maintenance whiners, they were never heavy lifters, rarely took on any extra task beyond the expected, and often weren't even doing the expected very well. Yet they would balk and complain, even as others around them worked harder, picked up the slack, went the extra mile. Others who were usually silent, often taken for granted.

Naturally, when I would mentally characterize them thus, it did not bring out the godliest traits in me.

And then it occurred to me that perhaps I should take folks at their word when they said they were busy. Not because I believed it, but because they believed it themselves. That is, just because they didn't appear busy by any standard I recognized, they felt busy by the standard that they did. They felt full up—and maybe, I realized, they weren't prevaricating, but reporting experience as they perceived it.

This, in turn, suggested to me a little parable about glassware. Some folks are shot glasses—they don't hold much and they overflow quickly, but no one would deny the delight that can come in that small container. On the other hand, some folks are Big Gulps. They have enormous capacity, a durable construction, and they can keep you hydrated all day. They rarely overflow and don't need to be refilled very often. The challenge, of course, is to learn to cherish them both—and all the other assorted glassware that makes up our lives. To know that a fully stocked kitchen has a use for everything.

So, sure, we should always endeavor to not exploit some and let others off the hook. But sometimes, as my late mother always said, "you've got to know what you're working with." The more important remaining question will always be, How does a faith-filled person handle the inevitable inequities and unfairnesses? How does one not value the quantity of work as the marker of the contribution of the individual? One way is acknowledging that our capacities vary widely (and, indeed, vary widely by the task at hand). And being okay with that. Living into that—difficult as our judgmental, always-comparing selves know only too well—seems like at least a small move away from exasperation, resentment, and comparison, and toward ever more grace to ourselves and those around us, no matter what we—and they—can hold.

I'll raise a glass to that.

LUCKY 13

If we began the chapter by rethinking about a story we feel we already know, I want to end the chapter with a biblical story I imagine we think rather little about: the story of the thirteenth apostle, Matthias. As we think about the narratives we need to define Christian vocation, his is an important one. Here's his story from Acts 1. After Jesus' ascension, the disciples returned to Jerusalem and discussed a replacement for their number. Peter set out the criteria:

> Therefore it is necessary to choose one of the men who have been with us the whole time the Lord Jesus was living among us, beginning from John's baptism to the time when Jesus was taken up from us. For one of these must become a witness with us of his resurrection." So they nominated two men: Joseph called Barsabbas (also known as Justus) and Matthias. Then they prayed, "Lord, you know everyone's heart. Show us which of these two you have chosen to take over this apostolic ministry, which Judas left to go where he belongs." Then they cast lots, and the lot fell to Matthias; so he was added to the eleven apostles. (Acts 1:21-26)

Matthias seems to come out of nowhere and disappear almost as quickly back into the text. He had been around Jesus' ministry from the very beginning, and yet this is the first—and last—we hear of him. No mentions in the gospels, no stories in Acts, no shout-outs in the New Testament letters. Who was this guy? Tradition, though it says more about him than Scripture, doesn't do much to answer that question. Interestingly, there are even disagreements about his name: unlike the triple-named specificity of "Joseph called Barsabbas (also known as Justus)," Matthias might really have been called Tolmai, according to Eusebius. Was he actually Zacchaeus (as Clement of Alexandria thought) or Barnabas (as a different Clement asserted)? Accounts of his ministry are equally at variance: Nicephorus's *Historia Ecclesiastica* tells of him serving in Judea, then modern-day Georgia; the *Synopsis of Dortheus* and the Coptic *Acts of Andrew and Matthias* both claim he preached in Ethiopia— sometimes among cannibals! And depending on whom you read, he died in one of the following ways:

- by crucifixion and was buried in the Roman fortress of Gonio (Nicephorus)
- by stoning in Jerusalem, where he was afterward beheaded (the French church historian Tillemont)
- of old age in either Sebastopolis (*Synopsis of Dortheus*) or Jerusalem (Hippolytus of Rome)

Whatever his story, you have to love a man whose saint day is considered the luckiest day of the year, particularly when you learn he is also the patron saint of perhaps the most random (and not terribly fortuitous) collection ever: alcoholics and those who live in Gary, Indiana, and Great Falls-Billings, Montana; tailors and carpenters; and smallpox. In many ways, then, he's a sort of "everyman" apostle. He could be anyone. He could have ministered anywhere.

Then again, I think that's the point. Notice the very simple criteria for selection:

Therefore it is necessary to choose one of the men who have been with us the whole time the Lord Jesus was living among

us, beginning from John's baptism to the time when Jesus was
taken up from us. For one of these must become a witness
with us of his resurrection. (Acts 1:21-22)

The essential part of a calling is the call to witness. In other words,
at heart we are not only invited into the story, we are to tell the story!
This is God's call throughout Scripture. Consider Isaiah 44:6-8:

This is what the LORD says—
        Israel's King and Redeemer, the LORD Almighty:
    I am the first and I am the last;
        apart from me there is no God. . . .
    Do not tremble, do not be afraid.
    Did I not proclaim this and foretell it long ago?
    You are my witnesses. Is there any God besides me?
    No, there is no other Rock; I know not one.

Imagine that: God calls on us to be a witness for him. As if he
needs support or proof! Clearly, the heavens and earth are already
declaring the glory of God. But amazingly, God seems to think
we're necessary to the project too.

And part of being a good witness is to give account of the whole
story: not just the act that saves us but the acts from which we are
saved. Studying the life of Jesus, particularly the events of Holy Week,
reminds us again of so many of the ways we fail in our relationships
with God and each other. Our disloyalties, our violence, our pride.
Our big talk and our lack of action. Our timidity and our jealousies.
Our misguided scheming and our imprudent plans. To not bear
witness to these realities would be to misrepresent the power of sin
that the Resurrection conquers. We must give witness to it all.

Thankfully, telling the sad tale of sin is only a part of our narrative task. It seems particularly significant to me that in the first
post-Resurrection sighting of Jesus, Jesus invites Mary Magdalene

and the other women to go and spread the good news. Given the status of women in first-century Palestine, Jesus' inclusion of women in the work of witness demonstrates the radical capaciousness of the gospel—this is a story for everyone to participate in and for everyone to tell. And like that passage in Isaiah, the New Testament resounds with the importance of our role as witnesses. In Acts 1:8, Jesus himself quite famously gives us this task: "But you will receive power when the Holy Spirit comes on you; and you will be my witnesses in Jerusalem, and in all Judea and Samaria, and to the ends of the earth."

The apostles, too, over and again assert the centrality of this role:

Acts 2:32: "God has raised this Jesus to life, and we are all witnesses of it."

Acts 3:15: "You killed the author of life, but God raised him from the dead. We are witnesses of this."

Acts 5:32: "We are witnesses of these things, and so is the Holy Spirit, whom God has given to those who obey him."

So how, then, do we continue to live into our call to be witnesses? One way is to listen to and retell the stories of those in that "great cloud of witnesses" (Heb 12:1). But this can't just be a remembrance of things past. If we truly believe that the power of the resurrection is the power to transform lives, then we need to give voice to God's work in our lives today. We do that part of our witnessing job by beholding and celebrating Christ in the lives of those around us. We often seem to forget that our great privilege as the church is in seeing the work of God in each other—and assisting with that work by noticing and encouraging it. So that each manifestation of the fruit of the Spirit—the joy in this person, the peace in that one, the faithfulness of another—might add praise to praise. Sometimes we don't even see these things ourselves until someone sees them for us. But the building up of love comes from seeing evidence of God's handiwork wherever we look—and we are essential to each other in this work. In *On Christian Teaching*, Saint Augustine puts it this way:

> The apostle Paul, no less, though cast to the ground and then enlightened by a divine voice from heaven, was sent to a human being to receive the sacrament of baptism and be joined to the church. And Cornelius the centurion, although an angel announced to him that his prayers had been heard and his acts of charity remembered, was nevertheless put under the tuition of Peter not only to receive the sacrament, but also to learn what should be the objects of his faith, hope, and love. All this could certainly have been done through an angel, but the human condition would be wretched indeed if God appeared unwilling to minister his words to human beings through human agency. . . . There would be no way for love, which ties people together in the bonds of unity, to make souls overflow and as it were intermingle with each other, if human beings learn nothing from other humans.[13]

So maybe Matthias's patronage isn't so random, after all. Maybe it gives us a window into the essence of who he is: your "average Joe" from sturdy but unglamorous places. A man committed to restoration, associated as he is with craftspeople who knit things together, whether in cloth or wood. A man, who having watched the Healer himself throughout his earthly ministry, understands the disfiguring consequences of addiction and disease. No wonder the other disciples nominated him.

The rest of his story doesn't really matter anyway. After all, we know the only thing that truly matters about him: he was a witness, ready to serve at the Spirit's call. May the same be said of us.

6

Our Little Systems

Our little systems have their day;
They have their day and cease to be:
They are but broken lights of thee,
And Thou, O Lord, art more than they.

ALFRED, LORD TENNYSON,
"PROLOGUE," *IN MEMORIAM*

THROUGHOUT HIS WORSHIPING LIFE at the Tree of Life synagogue, Dr. Jerry Rabinowitz always stood up each week during the prayer of mourning. Though it is considered more traditional to only stand when one is personally grieving, Dr. Rabinowitz steadfastly rose, nevertheless. He had no children himself, no descendants guaranteed to stand for him when his own death came, and so he stood, determined to represent those who had no one to stand for them. To commemorate and celebrate and offer respect for the wonder and dignity of each life as it was remembered in corporate prayer.

Then, Dr. Rabinowitz was one of eleven people killed at his synagogue in Pittsburgh by a white supremacist anti-Semite.

Who will rise for Dr. Rabinowitz?

Who will stand unshakable like that Tree of Life mirrored in the very synagogue itself?

It is not someone else's responsibility. The most important course I took in college was on the Holocaust, where our professor made painfully clear over sixteen weeks that the Holocaust happened not because of some kind of nameless evil concentrated in a few hands but because of deliberate choices made by everyday people systematically over centuries. No, that is too blandly put: by Christian people—who used their theology to justify these acts of hatred and suspicion, who intentionally made laws to dispossess and murder. For hundreds of years. And by Christian people, too, who deliberately chose not to respond on the scale and with the force required, who failed to speak out against injustices, small and large.

Who will rise for Dr. Rabinowitz? Who will say the names of the others lost that day?

Joyce Fienberg
Richard Gottfried
Rose Mallinger
Jerry Rabinowitz
Cecil and David Rosenthal
Bernice and Sylvan Simon
Daniel Stein
Melvin Wax
Irving Younger

Or the names of the precious children massacred at Newtown or of those beloved in the Lord killed at Charleston's Mother Emanuel Church? Who will remember and recite the litany of the literally thousands of people senselessly killed at their homes, their schools, their work, their places of worship, and elsewhere? Who will cry for justice?

"Evil," Flannery O'Connor once observed, "is not a problem to be solved, but a mystery to be endured."[1] If that is so, endurance certainly seems to have been strenuously called upon in these last years. I have a history degree (and I'm a Calvinist), so I'm not so naive as to not understand that such has it always been. And yet, the magnitude of violence, the hostile disregard for each other, the fragmentation and fraying of our social bonds, the persistent calamity of climate, the oppression of poverty and abusive systems of race and gender, and so much more, must be taken into account in the stories we tell. So far in this book, we've been considering how narrative can make us more capacious in our approach to God and to ourselves. But equally important is the way story can provide a corrective, a way to deal with despair, defeat, and death in a nuanced way.

It's why it bothers me so deeply when after most any tragedy, the press is full of pronouncements by self-identified Christians as to the reasons behind it. Such statements run the gamut from "I think we have turned our back on the Scripture and on God almighty, and he has allowed judgment to fall on us" to "We have systematically removed God from our schools, so should we be so surprised that schools would become a place of carnage?" Or the perennial favorite, "Everything happens for a reason" (so beautifully debunked by Duke University historian Kate Bowler, who after a stage four cancer diagnosis, examined that statement and, as her subtitle puts it, all the "other lies I've loved"). Or sometimes we get the unfortunate "God needed an angel." Such words flow after seemingly every tornado, flood, and hurricane. After plane crashes and car wrecks. After tsunamis and during pandemics. After any inexplicable horror—or worse, after anything of which the speaker disapproves. It is then we hear some Christian explain how [insert terrible thing here] is God's divine decree.

I'm tired of it. Not simply because I disagree with the theology but because of the hubris of it all. And the witness it gives of a faith that is presumptuous and triumphalist, smug and self-righteous. Every time I hear someone talk about God's will, God's judgment, God's whatever, I think of how Denise Levertov rues the "confident" way we speak of God's wishes, but then reminds us

Perhaps God wants
something quite different
Or nothing, nothing at all.[2]

How confidently indeed.

That's not to assert we can say nothing about God and God's
ways. I certainly don't believe that. But when we consider the
stories we tell, I nevertheless think we would do well to pay attention to narrative models that lead us toward humility and away
from self-congratulation. Toward bravery. In another poem,
"Goodbye to Tolerance," Levertov powerfully rejects the polite
neutrality of respectability, calling such things, evocatively,
"gobbets of language."

Genial poets, pink-faced
earnest wits—
you have given the world
some choice morsels,
gobbets of language presented
as one presents T-bone steak
and Cherries Jubilee.
Goodbye, goodbye,
            I don't care
if I never taste your fine food again,
neutral fellows, seers of every side.
Tolerance, what crimes
are committed in your name.

And you, good women, bakers of nicest bread,
blood donors. Your crumbs
choke me, I would not want
a drop of your blood in me, it is pumped
by weak hearts, perfect pulses that never

falter: irresponsive
to nightmare reality.

It is my brothers, my sisters,
whose blood spurts out and stops
forever
because you choose to believe it is not your business.

Goodbye, goodbye,
your poems
shut their little mouths,
your loaves grow moldy,
a gulf has split
          the ground between us,
and you won't wave, you're looking
another way.
We shan't meet again—
unless you leap it, leaving
behind you the cherished
worms of your dispassion,
your pallid ironies,
your jovial, murderous,
wry-humored balanced judgment,
leap over, un-
balanced? . . . then
how our fanatic tears
would flow and mingle
for joy. . . .[3]

Levertov's strong language not only describes what is wrong, but significantly, it centers the ones ("my brothers, my sisters / whose blood spurts out and stops forever") truly harmed. That is key.

That's true in stories like the book of Job, too. Job's friends provide an important lesson when they come and sit with him for seven days and seven nights *in silence* because "they saw that his pain was very great" (Job 2:13 NASB). It was when they began trying to explain Job's suffering—what *The Message* renders as "pious bluster" (Job 6:25 MSG)—that they go astray. Like them, we seem to get in trouble most when we open our mouths and speak for anyone but ourselves, assigning motives and interpretations far beyond our ability to reckon. Job's friends' first impulse was the right one: silence, presence with the victim, and lamentation.

As I write this, the Covid-19 pandemic is now entering its third calendar year, and I think of how important it has been when I've given time in my meetings with my students (virtually and in person) to take time to name our sadnesses: in leaving friends and plans behind, in cancellations and new systems of distancing, in illness and death. We've named the ways we missed being with each other and the experience of a "normal" class and all the changes in our larger university community. We speak of tremendous losses to our country and to our world. These are probably analogous to conversations you've been having with your workmates, your church friends, your wider communities. N. T. Wright powerfully articulates why these expressions are so necessary:

> It is no part of the Christian vocation, then, to be able to explain what's happening and why. In fact, it *is* part of the Christian vocation *not to be able* to explain—and to lament instead. As the Spirit laments within us, so we become, even in our self-isolation, small shrines where the presence and healing love of God can dwell. And out of that there can emerge new possibilities, new acts of kindness, new scientific understanding, new hope.[4]

I've thought a great deal about that phrase, "even in our self-isolation," since I live alone. Indeed, I have a friend who has long joked (pre-pandemic) that I'd "make a good shut-in." And I certainly acknowledge that my experience over these long years has had a very different contour than everyone struggling with the many demands of family life lived in and out of lockdowns and quarantine and the other demands of the Covid world. My experience is exactly the opposite: during the lockdown I never saw anyone except online or from a distance when walking. Since then, I don't entertain big groups like I used to, and I also rarely have anyone individually to the house. It has been very odd. I wondered how others handled it in the past: for example, my pastor reminded us that Lent parallels Jesus' forty days in the wilderness. I wonder how Jesus felt in *his* self-isolation? Or I think of the desert mothers and fathers who sought refuge alone? Or Julian of Norwich who, as a medieval anchorite, had herself walled into the church so she could practice solitude and spiritual contemplation. (Well, for the most part. She also had a window from which she could give advice and another through which she could observe the Mass.) Julian had lived through the plague and a severe illness and still wrote of the radical love of God, the way in which "all shall be well."[5] What, then, has come from my own time of isolation? As privileged as I am to have this time—when so many others do not—I want to be attentive to what I might gain from this gift.

One thing that seems critical is how lamentation focuses us on our brokenness and the brokenness of our world—and our absolute inability to ultimately fix any of it. T. S. Eliot's *Four Quartets* defines the problem like this:

So here I am . . .
Trying to use words, and every attempt
Is a wholly new start, and a different kind of failure
Because one has only learnt to get the better of words
For the thing one no longer has to say, or the way in which

One is no longer disposed to say it. And so each venture
Is a new beginning, a raid on the inarticulate
With shabby equipment always deteriorating
In the general mess of imprecision of feeling,
Undisciplined squads of emotion.[6]

We know this is true: we rarely have the right words at the right
moment, even at the best of times. The "shabby equipment" of expression, the "undisciplined squads of emotion" fail us. Partly, we have
other means of communication to supplement this failure. The comfort
and support of sitting at a funeral next to a dear one, for example. We
realize that words are not always necessary or even desired. Ideally, we
know our lives need to be a coordinated vocabulary of what we say and
what we do. And as these beautiful words from Nicholas Wolterstorff's
Lament for a Son—written after his son's accidental death—describe, it
is also in these imperfect cries that we importantly find the overarching
narrative of a God who was broken for us and for our salvation:

> How is faith to endure, O God, when you allow all this
> scraping and tearing on us? You have allowed rivers of blood
> to flow, mountains of suffering to pile up, sobs to become
> humanity's song—all without lifting a finger that we could see.
> You have allowed bonds of love beyond number to be pain-
> fully snapped. If you have not abandoned us, explain yourself.
>   We strain to hear. But instead of hearing an answer we
> catch sight of God himself scraped and torn. Through our
> tears we see the tears of God.[7]

Still, what I love about the *Four Quartets* is Eliot's deeply Christian
assertion that the effort is worth it: "For us, there is only the trying.
The rest is not our business."[8] These two simply stated sentences
have all sorts of freeing implications: Trying, not achieving, is the
goal. Perfection or full expression is not the goal, either. We don't

need to worry about the result. For Eliot, the effort of expression is vital. Knowing that we can't control the outcome, we are nevertheless to try and speak a word of comfort, sing a song of lament, raise a cry against injustice—even if, in the moment, that language fails to truly capture all that we feel or transform all that we wish could be different or changed or healed. "The rest is not our business" because we know whose business it is: Christ's. The Word made flesh, the model of perfectly embodied language.

WAVING, NOT DROWNING

Though some Christians might resist speaking out (too political, too aggressive), the nineteenth-century novelist Charlotte Brontë had no such difficulty. Brontë often seems to get characterized in the popular imagination as a "romance novelist" and, as such, one of the creative mothers of all the endlessly cheesy tales of courtship that have followed in the last two centuries. Though she (partly) takes love as her subject, that characterization is not really fair, especially given the level of critique that she offers of the constraints suffered as a result of the cultural and economic forces of her time. In fact, Brontë—a minister's daughter and a Sunday school teacher herself—explicitly saw herself speaking out of a prophetic tradition—with the fiery rhetoric to match.

Brontë's *Jane Eyre* was a literary sensation when it was published in 1847, becoming an immediate bestseller. But some critics were quick to point to what they saw as the "pre-eminently anti-Christian" nature of the book: its claim for equality—spiritual, emotional, financial, relational—between men and women, its insistence on God's call to active vocation for all, and its audacious claim that a "plain Jane" deserves an autobiography. Brontë, they said, was stirring up "discontent" and her writings more generally, wrote Matthew Arnold, were full of "hunger, rebellion, and rage." [9]

Charlotte Brontë was having none of it. In her preface to the
second edition of *Jane Eyre*, she strikes back and characterizes her
critics as the "timorous or carping few who doubt the tendency of
such books as *Jane Eyre*, in whose eyes whatever is unusual is
wrong; whose ears detect in each protest against bigotry—that
parent of crime—an insult to piety, that regent of God on earth."
I love here how she shrinks her critics down to whiny complainers—
but more importantly, how she calls out the way that "protest
against bigotry" (that is, naming systemic wrongs) is not irreligious.
Instead, channeling the powerful voice of the sagest of Victorian
sages, she witheringly dismisses these critics and calls them out on
what she sees as their hypocrisy, closed-mindedness, and ultimately,
their lack of true understanding about what Christianity teaches:

> I would suggest to such doubters certain obvious distinctions;
> I would remind them of certain simple truths.
>
> Conventionality is not morality. Self-righteousness is not
> religion. To attack the first is not to assail the last. To pluck
> the mask from the face of the Pharisee is not to lift an impious
> hand to the Crown of Thorns.
>
> These things and deeds are diametrically opposed: they
> are as distinct as is vice from virtue. Men too often confound
> them: they should not be confounded. Appearance should
> not be mistaken for truth; narrow human doctrines that only
> tend to elate and magnify a few should not be substituted for
> the world-redeeming creed of Christ. There is—I repeat it—a
> difference; and it is a good, and not a bad action to mark
> broadly and clearly the line of separation between them.
>
> The world may not like to see these ideas dissevered, for it
> has been accustomed to blend them, finding it convenient to
> make external show pass for sterling worth—to let white-
> washed walls vouch for clean shrines. It may hate him who

dares to scrutinize and expose—to raze the gilding and show base metal under it—to penetrate the sepulchre and reveal charnel relics: but hate as it will, it is indebted to him.[10]

In these forceful words, Brontë unapologetically asserts that critique is an essential duty of the Christian, who like Christ, must expose the "charnel relics" in the whitened "sepulchre." Significantly, with her rallying cry, "conventionality is not morality," she points to the still pervasive problem of performative Christianity— of acting as expected externally, of upholding "narrow human doctrines" which oppress the many—while not being willing to brave the disdain and rejection that comes with calling things out. The silences of complicity that she condemns are ones that still need condemning today.

And if that weren't enough—she provides a model for us by concluding the passage with an implicit comparison between herself and the Old Testament prophet Micaiah—and perhaps more damningly, between Ahab and her Victorian detractors. It is not she who is "un-Christian" but people like the evil king Ahab and his "sycophant" adviser—those who trade truth for power. "Ahab did not like Micaiah because he never prophesied good concerning him but only evil; probably he liked the sycophant son of Chenaanah better. Yet Ahab might have escaped a bloody death had he but stopped his ears to flattery and opened them to faithful counsel."[11] To speak out even when it is unpopular, then, Charlotte Brontë reminds us, is the duty of the prophet. Brontë's confident use of the Bible here—figuring herself as both Christlike and prophet-like—shows us a writer who used her faith to authorize her speaking against the injustices of her time. And it models—both in its charge and in its warning—the hard necessities that come with so doing.

Brontë is one nineteenth-century model. Another is the poet Christina Rossetti who also offered critiques of Victorian society, but who I want to highlight here because she also speaks hard truths about herself and the struggles of the Christian life. If we think of Brontë as the macro level, Rossetti can stand in for micro-level critique: she is a master at the lament for the self. Though Rossetti's critical reputation has always been high, many critics have struggled with her unwavering Christian commitment and her huge output of religious verse, particularly in the later part of her career. Her poems of romantic transgression and renunciation have usually found a more appreciative audience in the wider academy, perhaps because a nonreligious audience finds them easier to relate to than her intense, often unrelentingly self-critical religious examinations. But it is this latter group of poems that I find much to identify with, no doubt because I know only too well the ways I myself fall short every day in living out the faith, hope, and love of Christ's calling—and how much we often want to keep that reckoning out of our stories.

In her poem "Who Shall Deliver Me," for example, Rossetti's speaker is fierce and fiercely honest, not only in her self-diagnosis of her failings, but in her self-awareness, even self-consciousness, of these failings.[12] In classic Romans 7 fashion, the speaker—who definitely knows better and certainly wants to do better—nevertheless, cannot. She pleads: "God strengthen me to bear myself / That heaviest weight of all to bear / Inalienable weight of care." And then several lines later, she goes on to accuse: "Myself, arch-traitor to myself / My hollowest friend, my deadliest foe / My clog whatever road I go." Similarly, in her poem "Good Friday," Rossetti presents a speaker who is a Christian but who doesn't feel like she's "supposed to," experiencing a numbness to the Easter story of Christ's sacrifice. The speaker knows that she *should* feel something—like the women at the cross, like Peter, like the dying thief—but honestly feels nothing.

"GOOD FRIDAY"

Am I a stone and not a sheep,
That I can stand, O Christ, beneath Thy cross,
To number drop by drop Thy blood's slow loss,
And yet not weep?

Not so those women loved
Who with exceeding grief lamented Thee;
Not so fallen Peter weeping bitterly;
Not so the thief was moved;

Not so the Sun and Moon
Which hid their faces in the starless sky,
A horror of great darkness at broad noon —
I, only I.

Yet give not o'er,
But seek Thy sheep, true Shepherd of the flock
Greater than Moses, turn and look once more,
And smite a rock.[13]

Victorian women were generally praised for being pious, even if it was performative. Rossetti utterly rejects that, writing poems where speakers are honest about their spiritual states, even when they are unflattering. These speakers do not want to let themselves off the hook, or to blame others. They bravely name their failures. But in both poems, as in Wolterstorff's above, their cries of individual brokenness are met with a recognition that they are not lost to the grace of God (even if being found might prove painful, too, as a rock being smote). That's powerful too.

Perhaps we also need to find better examples of how to narrate our response to the sufferings of others. In the twentieth-century poet Stevie Smith's most famous poem, "Not Waving but Drowning," we begin with what seems a simple, though tragic, scene: a dead man who wasn't heard when he cried for help.[14] Ostensibly, he has had a drowning accident. Indeed, in the middle stanza, the observers on the beach ("they") give all sorts of reasons (excuses?) for the dead man's state—he liked to "lark" about; the "too cold" sea overwhelmed him. Obviously, "they" imply no one's at fault that he wasn't saved, least of all any of them.

But the poem makes clear it's not the coldness of the sea. In the title, in the last two lines of the first stanza, and then more emphatically in the final stanza, the dead man repeats that through his whole life he has felt adrift and alienated—the environment around him "too cold always." No one hears him because no one listens. Worse, his very cry for help is misread: he was "not waving but drowning."

I think of this poem often: Who will I encounter today whose "larking" hides a deep void, an inner freezing? Who is drifting "too far out"? Who is feeling overwhelmed by the waves? How can I make sure that I pay attention so that the wish for help doesn't get misinterpreted as a wave? It's terribly difficult—and I know I'm no lifeguard. But if nothing else, I know I need to be intentional in making sure that the people important to me—whether as colleagues or students, friends or family—understand that they never swim alone. That their story is heard.

Finally, we need to find ways to talk well about death, often the topic most prone to either sentimentality, bad theology, or both. Yet a rich tradition of literature that treats death well awaits the reader. This is just an example that has been meaningful to me. You see, though Easter was a huge deal in my family, we never did Ash Wednesday when I was growing up. No service, no imposition of ashes. And although my parents adored the Advent season (during which we had many family traditions, including daily lighting of our Advent wreath and daily chocolate eating from our Advent calendars),

Lent was completely ignored. (We still had daily family devotions as we always did, lest you think we were complete spiritual slackers.) We didn't do Fat/Shrove Tuesday either—so no paczkis or pancakes or whatever celebratory foods people eat on such occasions. Between Christmas and Easter was simply the long stretch of winter. As an adult, I've engaged more with the church calendar, but Ash Wednesday has even now never been something to which I've attended much. In fact, I usually only remember that the day has arrived after my forehead-besmudged students show up in class.

And it's probably in part because a reminder of my inevitable dusty ending is not something I am keen to contemplate. When my mother died unexpectedly, my family had to scramble to purchase a burial plot since my parents—being only middle-aged—hadn't gotten around to selecting one yet. It was a hard enough process given the suddenness of my mother's death, but in some ways the real kicker was when the cemetery director asked my father if he'd like to buy a space for himself while he was purchasing one for my mother. A graveyard twofer, if you will. I get that such is the business of funerals, but I remember thinking at the time, *Must we? Do I have to face both of my parents' deaths at the very same moment?*

The answer, of course, is yes. With each passing year and the ever-increasing loss of relatives and friends, that *yes* grows only more insistent. To visit the grave and see inscribed both the name of my dead mother and of my living father is to have mortality made tangible—and undeniable. But I wonder if Ash Wednesday might be more than a reminder of mortality, more than a lamenting of our sinfulness (though that alone would make it fully worthwhile). I wonder if it might be akin to the poem by Jane Kenyon, "Otherwise."[15] In that poem, Kenyon, with her attention to the "luminous particular," catalogs the wonders of the average day—ending each section with the comment, "it might have been otherwise." But these daily wonders come into focus for her *because* of the "otherwisely" nature of life: that is, that it has a preordained end. That fact doesn't make life less good—instead, it helps illuminate the goodness.

Kenyon's husband, the poet Donald Hall, had a long, distinguished career, including a stint as US Poet Laureate. Jane Kenyon died of leukemia in April 1995—and in the succeeding years, Hall was immersed in the exploration of his grief. Five years after Kenyon's death, Hall first published "Distressed Haiku" in *The Atlantic*, a masterpiece of the navigations of the grieving.[16] Maybe because my own mother had died quite suddenly only a year before, I found Hall's lines especially meaningful. I still do.

But while Kenyon's poem "Otherwise" is about the preparation for death, Hall's is about living in the aftermath of loss. It moves in lament through its first ten lines from Hall's desire to be near Kenyon again, if only at her grave, to the remembrance of their anniversary and his emotional exhaustion:

In a week or ten days
the snow and ice
will melt from Cemetery Road.

I'm coming! Don't move!

*

Once again it is April.
Today is the day
we would have been married
twenty-six years.
I finished with April
halfway through March.

And then comes the emotional gut-punch in the center stanza of the poem, one of the most honest articulations of grief I've ever read, a line that comes to mind often:

> You think that their
> dying is the worst
> thing that could happen.
> Then they stay dead.

And yet, even in unvarnished bereavement, the last two stanzas move toward hope, toward the miraculous upending of everything expected (this poem was written before the Red Sox were finally redeemed in their quest for a World Series championship).

> Will Hall ever write
> lines that do anything
> but whine and complain?
>
> In April the blue
> mountain revises
> from white to green.
>
> The Boston Red Sox win
> a hundred straight games.
> The mouse rips
> the throat of the lion
>
> and the dead return.

The cheeky self-chiding, "Will Hall ever write lines that do anything but whine and complain," particularly in light of the image of the mountain's Easter-like rebirth, signals a recognition that all is not lost. April may indeed be the "cruelest month," as T. S. Eliot reckons in "The Wasteland," with its mixing of "memory and desire," the yearning for those who are gone and remain gone, but it is also (often) the month of the resurrection when "the dead return." We must name the reality of death to grasp the joy and power of Easter.

OUR LITTLE SYSTEMS

Whatever the loss, I think we need to come to terms with the stories we tell ourselves about that loss.

When I went to college, I received a scholarship called the President's Associates scholarship. It was an incredible gift, paying for my tuition and my books as well as providing a stipend. As the name implies, we also had opportunities to meet donors and community members as part of the award, and several times a year, the small group of us PAs were invited to have dinner at our university president's home.

At the reception before the first dinner I attended as a freshman, a very elderly man came over and chatted with me. Warm and welcoming, he asked me all sorts of questions about myself. And when I asked him what *he* did, he replied offhandedly that he was "just a retired science professor." Kind and unpretentious, he was interested in who I was and what I was going to do—and at every dinner after that over my four years, he always sought me out, asked me for an update, told me his latest pun, and often sat with me during the meal.

Except I'm not telling you the whole story.

After I met this professor the first time, our university president came over and said, "Oh, I see you've met Clyde Tombaugh."

"Yes," I responded, "he seems really nice." The president's wry smile told me I was missing something.

"Did you know he discovered the planet Pluto?" The president did not seem surprised when I admitted professor Tombaugh had never mentioned it—he hadn't even mentioned he was in astronomy. Instead, here was one of a handful of people in world history to ever discover a planet asking freshman me about how my life and studies were going.

And that kindness is important. Because, as you probably know, Pluto was demoted in 2006 to "dwarf planet." It saddened me to think that professor Tombaugh would probably become just a trivia question: that guy who discovered a planet that really wasn't one after all. The scientist who lost his planet.

I was pleased, then, at the excitement when recent NASA excursions went by Pluto. Pleased not because of the possible scientific advances but because I had liked professor Tombaugh so much and I was happy that his discovery was getting attention. It seems to me, though, that such a response isn't a very faithful one. Because it meant that professor Tombaugh's value lay only in his achievements, not in what was true about him: that he was a lovely human being, whatever else he had done or discovered.

After all, what happens when we lose our "planets"? What happens when our achievements are surpassed or diminished (as they always are) or are simply not as important as they once were? What happens when illness leaves us radically changed? When a beloved person dies and the landscape becomes disorientingly unfamiliar? When a retirement happens before we've figured out who we are without work?

What kind of story have we cultivated to tell us who we are, especially when the planet we discovered ceases to be the defining fact of our narrative? I love the way Tennyson gets at the question in *In Memoriam*:

Our little systems have their day
They have their day and cease to be
They are but broken lights of Thee
And Thou, oh Lord, art more than they.[17]

Our "little systems"—be they our bodily systems eventually winding down with age, our philosophical systems being surpassed by the newest "ism" or "ology," our technological systems grown slow and unresponsive—can only go so far, can only give limited luminosity. Our stories themselves, then, are only "broken lights." We need something brighter, something more illuminating.

STEADY 'TIL SUNSET

I claimed earlier in this chapter that one of the important aspects of narrating brokenness is that it emphasizes "our absolute inability to ultimately fix any of it." That seems worth exploring a little further, especially since it flies in the face of can-do American exceptionalism and certain kinds of Christian overconfidence.

The intermittent chirping woke me up a little after 5:00 a.m.

At first, the timing of the cheeps was spaced far enough apart that I could never get a good handle on which room exactly the noise was coming from, even as I wandered around in the dark trying to figure it out. It didn't help that I wasn't at home but visiting an out-of-town friend.

With nothing obviously on fire, I realized that the warning beeps were the batteries in the smoke detector bidding adieu. I kept searching—but in vain. Turns out, even if I had found the offending device, I wouldn't have been able to do anything about it anyway. It seems there was a code that had to be entered that I had no way of knowing.

Of course, I could have just gone and woken up my friend, sleeping on the upper floor at the opposite end of the house. But I didn't want to. I figured if she couldn't hear it, there was no reason for both of us to lose sleep.

And as I lay back down, it occurred to me that the still-beeping alarm was a metaphor. (Not a perfect one, I realize, but it was 5:00 a.m. and I'm an English professor, so I tend to think lots of things are probably metaphors.) I thought about the hard seasons in which so many people I knew were finding themselves. And I wrestled again with how we help each other through them. We know that something is wrong (there's an alarm going off, after all). Maybe it's a big something (the house is burning down) or maybe small (the batteries need changing), but whatever it is, we clearly hear the need for help. Yet it's not our house, and so we can't fix it—even if we want to.

As usual, it made me think about who might serve as good models. About Samwise Gamgee in *The Lord of the Rings: The Return of the King*.[18] Arguably the strongest character throughout the trilogy, he repeatedly wants to ease Frodo's burden and carry the ring for him. But Frodo always refuses. Finally, as they make their final ascent to destroy the ring, Sam understands: he can't carry the ring, but he can carry Frodo and in so doing bear his burden too. Like Sam, we err when we believe that we can solve the problems of our friends or that our "superior" strength can shield them from the difficulties they encounter.

But maybe there are ways of thinking constructively about the right ways to help.

I've never been a fan of the poem "Footprints." In fact, that's an understatement. Any of my students reading this will no doubt laugh at the blandness of this comment since I often use this "poem" as my shorthand for the trite verse that too often passes for "Christian art."

Still, I got to thinking about the poem after I visited an out-of-town friend after a winter storm hit and made driving in her small town impossible for a couple of days. When it was time to give her dog his exercise and we couldn't go to one of their usual spots, we walked to a nearby field—where he romped jubilantly about, even though it was deeply blanketed. My friend, too, moved effortlessly through the snow, striding easily along with her dog.

I, on the other hand, was not quite such a picture of gracefulness. Though I was wearing boots, I found it a hard slog through the knee-high snow. My stubby legs just could not seem to keep up. And the Big Bad Wolf himself would have envied my huffing and puffing as I strove to maintain the pace set by my fantastically fit friend.

Until I realized that I didn't have to keep up on my own. And it didn't have to be a slog. All I had to do was put my feet in the tracks already made by my friend. Rather wonderfully, we wear the same shoe size: seven and a half. But I'm quite clear that that's where the similarity ends: I could wear the best footwear in the world, and I am still sadly out of shape. But once I let my better-disciplined, in-shape friend take the lead and didn't struggle to match a pace I was incapable of, she made it possible for me to go farther and faster than I could have on my own. Just as importantly, by being able to follow her, she kept me out and going longer than I probably would have done by myself. Indeed, walking with her always inspires me to want to get into better shape so that I can walk more, especially if that means walking more with her.

Much as the sappiness of "Footprints" annoys me, I'm not denying, as the poem envisions, that there are times that God carries us. But out in that snowy field, having my path made by my friend, I remembered again that discipleship is literally about following behind someone we acknowledge as greater than ourselves, someone from whom we know we need to learn, someone we need to emulate. And realizing the peace that can come from acknowledging our flabby spiritual condition—and from knowing the God who has made the way for us already.

On the hallway that runs by my office are portraits of people who have served in the English department through the years—most retired, some sadly died before retirement came. Often, a picture catches my eye as I walk to class, and I think *big shoes to fill*. But I've come to realize it's not about metaphorically wearing their shoes, not about trying to be as good as those who came before. Rather it's that we can rejoice in how they have contributed to the path before us, in how they have given us places to put our own feet, even if for a time, before we continue the path for those coming behind us.

Or maybe there's a paradigm to be had in the story relayed in Exodus 17. Here, Moses must keep his arms raised to ensure victory over the Amalekites, but as his arms grow tired and he lowers them, the tide of the battle shifts. Though no one else can take Moses' place doing this hard work, Aaron and Hur hold Moses' hands "steady till sunset" (Ex 17:12) and in so doing give him the strength to get through.

Presence and support often seem very weak indeed, particularly when compared to the prophetic voice of someone like Brontë. I want to fix it and fix it now. I want to fight the battles and protect those I love from difficulty and despair, guilt, and grief. Both are needed, so what do we do? Besides the important step of acknowledging our inability to take away whatever is causing the alarm, we can decide to be present even while the alarm is sounding. To not let the alarm scare us or cause us to run away. Even if that means losing some sleep in the process or being discomfited by the sound of the distress.

PIRSUMEI NISA

In honor of Dr. Rabinowitz, I close this chapter with a consideration of Hanukkah, the Jewish Festival of Lights. Many of you are no doubt aware that it commemorates two miracles at once: the Maccabees' triumph over their Greek oppressors as well as the discovery of oil that seemed sufficient for only one night but burned instead for eight.

Whoever we are, we are living in a period of hard, dark years. We're looking for illumination. And while acknowledging that this holiday must have its own integrity for Jews celebrating it, thinking about Hanukkah might be instructive for Christians too.

Freedom. Though Hanukkah is not one of the major Jewish holidays, I find it fascinating that scholars often discuss a connection between Passover, Purim, and Hanukkah because each marks the move from bondage to liberty. It's a theme that runs through the entire Jewish year: God's demonstrated desire to save his people again and again. In each of the stories, the situation seems hopeless, the government cruel and relentless, the way out obscure. But that's never the last word. As importantly, this freedom comes through people raised up—Moses, Esther, the Maccabees—who were willing to act, usually at their peril, to bring about justice. It's no wonder, then, that Mary in her Magnificat—the moment that signals God's ultimate rescue—invokes this same powerful theme, recalling the long history of divine emancipation. Listen to her words again:

> He has shown strength with his arm;
>> he has scattered the proud in the thoughts of their hearts.
> He has brought down the mighty from their thrones,
>> and lifted up the lowly;
> he has filled the hungry with good things,
>> and sent the rich away empty.
> He has helped his servant Israel,
>> in remembrance of his mercy,
> according to the promise he made to our ancestors,
>> to Abraham and to his descendants forever. (Lk 1:51-55)

Abundance. When the Maccabees regained the Temple, they found that it had been largely desecrated. And they could find only one remaining container of oil that had received priestly blessing, which they did not think would last beyond the day. But just as their small band of rebels had received enough to defeat the colonizing Greeks, so too did the oil parallel God's lavish provision. We only need to show up to the temple to desire worship—and God will supply the rest. Beyond what we can imagine.

Sanctity. Significantly, the candles that are lit each evening for Hanukkah are not to be used for any other purposes, such as lighting the room. I'm not sure the same can be said metaphorically for our Christmas preparations. Too many articles have been written about the commercialization of Christmas—but nothing ever changes. Except maybe for the worse—with some folks' demands for businesses to participate fully in that commercialization: Isn't it a bit ludicrous that Starbucks has to offer just the right cup every year? That "Merry Christmas" must be the salutation when I buy celery? Might it not be nicer to actually have a religious celebration—and not expect the barista or bagger to participate with me at their work? To keep the candle, as it were, for only the thing for which it was intended?

Witness. And yet, I'm not arguing for absence or apology for the claims of the holiday. For me, one of the most affecting lessons of Hanukkah is the injunction *pirsumei nisa*, typically rendered as "publicize the miracle." Historically, the rabbis were very clear that when the candles are lit, they should be visible to everyone who passes by. In fact, they provide specific directions as to things like the time of day or the placement in the window to optimize people's viewing, so that your neighbors should have no doubt of what you were celebrating.

In this season of growing darkness, I wonder how we as Christians choose to publicize the miracle *we* proclaim. If it's not leading to greater illumination—to a greater light—we might want to rethink how we're doing it. How can we name the miracle, not as a simple fix but as an abiding truth?

Small Steps at Very Great Cost

We were made to understand it would be
Terrible. Every small want, every niggling urge,
Every hate swollen to a kind of epic wind.

Livid, the land, and ravaged, like a rageful
Dream. The worst in us having taken over
And broken the rest utterly down.

A long age
Passed. When at last we knew how little
Would survive us—how little we had mended

Or built that was not now lost—something
Large and old awoke. And then our singing
Brought on a different manner of weather.

Then animals long believed gone crept down
From trees. We took new stock of one another.
We wept to be reminded of such color.

Tracy K. Smith, "An Old Story"

In "An Old Story" by recent US Poet Laureate Tracy K. Smith, the world is destroyed by selfish, hateful, angry people— "the worst in us having taken over / And broken the rest utterly down."[1] In these words I hear echoes of W. B. Yeats's modernist diagnosis of a society where "[t]he best lack all conviction, while the worst / Are full of passionate intensity."[2] Both descriptions sound a lot like America today. Though Smith's poem eventually moves to a vision of restoration, I want us to initially pause in this chapter on the vision presented in the poem's first six lines, and to consider the intersection of story and community. How do the stories we tell affect the communities we inhabit?

On the one hand, there is a long-running debate in the field of English about the power of literature to, somehow, inherently improve readers. If you hang around long enough with literary types, you'll hear the assertion that story (or maybe "beauty" or "art") will save us or at least make us better and more empathetic—as if the mere act of reading and looking will transform our otherwise self-centered lives. Or for some, it's reading the "right" things: in the nineteenth century, for example, Matthew Arnold hoped that if society couldn't be united around a common religious belief, that an education with a core of "the best that has been thought and said" (a cultural canon to replace the biblical one) might be the answer.[3] There's still pressure for people to read the "right" things, though what they might be is always quite contentious. Or, another argument goes, perhaps one could become better by displacing the self in identification with a literary other, and thus make such a move in life as well (that is, not seeing oneself as the center of the story). A related corollary of this assertion is that we might achieve empathy for another by reading literature with characters unlike ourselves in some way.

Now, I certainly think there is some merit to these arguments: my own outlook has been tremendously expanded by reading widely and deeply (as this book attests). In recent years, it's been a privilege for me to consider with my students Yaa Gyasi's convicting saga of the African diaspora, *Homegoing*, or Min Jin Lee's powerful multigenerational novel of Koreans in Japan, *Pachinko*, or Tayari Jones's *An American Marriage*, and Bryan Stevenson's *Just Mercy* on mass incarceration. Hearing stories from a multiplicity of voices and perspectives is always a good that should be rigorously pursued. Representation matters. That is not debatable.

On the other hand, I'm still somewhat hesitant about the claim of *saving*. After all, books—even the very best ones—are not magical in and of themselves, and being well-read or highly in tune with great literature (however it is defined) is no guarantee that one has learned humility, readerly or otherwise. And reading about others unlike us doesn't guarantee we have learned to center a story other than our own. The frequent move to see literature as relatable (i.e., this character seems like me) can mean that a reader has flattened the story to emphasize similarities over differences. And reading widely is certainly no stay against inhumanity: after all, one needs only remember how highly cultured pre–World War II German society was, even as it systematically pursued the Holocaust. No, granting as I did that reading diversely is absolutely necessary, I think a better claim is that paying attention to the *way* we read—the strategies, the presuppositions, for example—and the *why* we read can help us determine if we are indeed pursuing "nourishing narratives" and moving toward more Christlike ways of viewing the world. This is a readerly take on 1 Corinthians 13: we can read all the "right" things, but if we aren't reading with charity and humility, with a desire to elevate another perspective, it's the equivalent of the "clanging gong" (1 Cor 13:1). Instead, how can we embrace reading principles—including the selection of what we read and how—that help us, as Saint Augustine urged, to build up love of neighbor and God?

ALL THAT WE BEHOLD

Certainly, Christians do not assert that it is belief in the Bible that saves them, but rather that it is Christ and his redemptive work. Nevertheless, Christ's work is relayed in a story that is supposed to undergird our community life together. That seems like it would be a unifying narrative that could provide direction, at least for people who identify as Christians. But it's not as easy as that: during the Covid-19 pandemic, I've struggled to understand fellow Christians who are responding so differently than I am, even as I remind myself that they have heard the same stories from the Bible that I have. It's made me wonder how we think about our Christian neighbor.

During the months of lockdown I found that I actually loved staying home. Despite what most people seem to think, being a childless spinster has a great many benefits—and one of them is already being used to spending a good deal of time alone. I relished getting rid of the many "shoulds" in my life, being able to focus on work, and enjoying the quiet and comforts of home.

I was feeling especially grateful one morning. My living room–dining room combination features a cathedral ceiling, and in the dining room, a very large window stretches from floor to ceiling. Through the window, I can see a lovely garden and, unfolding beyond, the street opposite in our peaceful little neighborhood. The woman who lived in my condo before me planted an incredible array of flowers, so throughout the summer I have a succession of gorgeous blooms. Facing eastward, the window is also the portal of the sun, which that particular morning was positively cascading into my dining room. In response, I began to have what the nineteenth-century writers I study might have called a positive revelry. Everything struck me as just delightful: my house, the morning, the garden, the whole dang day ahead. Now I tend toward the Tiggerish anyway, but my prayers that morning were joyfully exuberant—thanking God for seen and unseen, the wonders through my window and all the other gifts of friends and family and all good things.

And then it happened. Just as a line from Wordsworth's "Tintern Abbey"—"all that we behold is full of blessing"—flitted through my mind (and yes, this really happens to English professors), something else appeared in the window: coming down the sidewalk in front of my house was an all-campus colleague, sauntering along, who drives me sort of nuts. A person who has been mean to friends, is exasperating to deal with—not really in my top twenty favorites, let's say. Definitely not someone who was making the "Happy Summer Morning Praise to Jesus" list.

I burst out laughing. God's sense of humor was impeccable, as always. Seriously: "All that we behold is full of blessing"? Oh really, Miss Merry Sunshine? All?

I realized that I had been enjoying the quarantine because I had the luxury of not having to deal with people up-close. It's easy to love the world in the abstract through the glass of a window (or of a computer screen). I can't say that it wasn't a nice break—but it's bad spiritual practice. It put me in mind of a Chrome extension from several years ago called Unbaby.me that changed all pictures of babies in your Facebook newsfeed (seemingly people were sick of seeing their friends' endless stream of baby pictures) to pictures of cats or dogs or bacon or rainbows or whatever you choose, instead. A program like Unbaby.me plays into our deepest fantasies of control: If only the world looked like how I wanted it to look. If only I could block out that annoying person I have to work or worship with. If only I could substitute songs I want to sing and in a genre I want to sing them in at church. If only I didn't have to know about that person's feelings about Covid or politics or faith. Is there an app for that?

We say we desire community, but if we look closely, we prefer when it's in our own super-customizable way. As social media has continued to expose more and more about our family and friends' thinking and commitments, it's been harder to know how to deal with what we end up seeing. But the heart of Christianity, after all, *is* dealing with people, is about embodying Christ's love. It's always easier to not love our neighbor—our real neighbor, not some theoretical one. It's always easier to not engage in a Christlike way with all their unloveliness and annoyingness and wrong-headedness, even as we struggle to remember our identical condition. Easier to stay in the happy sunlight of our own sweet spaces, spaces we control and in which we feel comfortable. Or metaphorically replacing babies with bacon. So how can we do better—when every natural instinct leads us exactly the other way?

"IN ESSENTIALS, LIBERTY"

It had been one of those incredibly busy days, and when I finally got home, I found an email from a staff member at the college. He wondered why I hadn't attended a breakfast his department had coordinated for some of our incoming students that morning. Though his email was temperately worded, I could tell that he was not pleased that I had been absent.

Simple, I responded (trying to be equally temperate): the breakfast was optional. The email I had received had said it was—or at least implied it. I had taken them at their word that our required work was advising these same students in the afternoon. That I had done—and gladly. The breakfast sounded nice, but it was one thing I was glad was noncompulsory in an already-busy day.

Turns out, though, my colleague had a different sense of what optional meant. "To be honest," he wrote me in reply, "I'm not sure how optional the breakfast really is." Though the emails I had received had taken a tone of invitation (instead of directive or demand), the breakfast was, for him and his staff, clearly an indispensable part of the day. Now, my colleague is a good-hearted man, and his office works hard to make students welcome at our college, so in our email exchange, we were able to quickly see how unspoken assumptions had influenced the way we each had interpreted our expectations of the situation. But our exchange reminded me of how often we react to each other—in judgment, in criticism, in frustration—based on things we implicitly believe are obvious and fundamental, even though we seldom actually ever communicate them—or sometimes communicate, intentionally or not, the very opposite.

I've always been fond of the formulation, variously attributed to Saint Augustine or John Wesley (and a few others): "in essentials, unity; in non-essentials, liberty; in all things, charity." The problem comes, of course, in the definition of *essentials*. What are they? How do we communicate them? In what things must we work toward unity, in what toward liberty? How are we rigorously examining and articulating the warrants that undergird our beliefs and actions, instead of only critiquing people who think differently? Because without a clear sense of these, we'll continue to waste more time than we should on kerfuffles that distract us and drain the energy we have available for the work of servanthood that lies before us.

In such a polarized time, I realize this work of articulating and interrogating is not easy. But at least expecting the adherence to these principles as a goal for those of us in the wider Christian community to attempt, even in a small way, is a start. This is true whether it's debates about politics or Covid or sexuality or all the other issues that have fractured us. Actually, my question is really broader than any one divisive issue. Instead I want to ask, What is the church's witness, even (or especially) in the midst of asking hard questions and facing tough decisions? From within: What happens when our Christian neighbor becomes our enemy? How do we actually love them—since the call to love neighbor and enemy are both Christ's command? Externally: How do we ensure that folks see the tender grace of God, even when we are at odds with each other? Can we argue well? How do we show the winsomeness of a Savior who cares for the "least of these" when we are being disagreeable with one another or asserting power? When I lived in Japan for several years in high school, every time you left the base, you were greeted with this sign:

You are now leaving the Base.

You represent America.

Act accordingly.

I wonder if we need a similar reminder at church: of the God we represent in our essential identity and the actions and attitudes that responsibility demands. How do we testify to the Spirit's leading when it is clear that we feel we know the truth already?

And when we think about defining essentials, it's difficult to not narrate them through strongly denominational approaches. Our affirmation of a "holy catholic church" can sound a little hollow. As an Army brat, I think my experience in going to the "General Army Protestant" service each week as a child gives me a different view and a stronger appreciation for difference than many may have. In the chapel, I worshiped each week with people from a range of Protestant denominations. This meant that in our service,

we worshiped together, but simultaneously we also worshiped according to what our own traditions dictated. For example, people
took Communion while seated, while kneeling in the pew, or
while kneeling at the altar. We had infant baptisms, and we had
infant dedications, and we had infant christenings. We sang
hymns that ran the gamut. But the result was not some kind of
inoffensive pablum that obscured all theological flavor; the result
was an experience where I learned to respect the differences of my
fellow Christians, even while worshiping side by side—as the
church universal—with them each week. Like a prism, each
Christian tradition refracted the plenitude of God, helping me see
ever more ways to love God in heart, soul, mind, and strength.
But we also were clear about what bound us together.

As importantly, we shared the sanctuary with our Catholic
brothers and sisters—something vital, I believe. And not just the
same sanctuary but the same altar. On that altar was a curious thing:
a unique cross. For the Protestant service, the cross presented a
plain metal front to the congregation. But for the Mass that same
cross was turned around to reveal the figure of Jesus hanging on it.

Every time I describe that cross, it generates a good deal of
chuckling. And I admit, there's a certain amount of whimsy in a
"flippy cross." On the other hand, it has always been for me a powerful image. The Catholic emphasis on the crucifixion, the Protestant emphasis on the resurrection: the redemptive work of Christ
represented in one object. When I recite the Apostles' Creed and I
affirm the "holy catholic church," then, what I am really affirming
is that I need as many eyes as possible to help me fully see and
deeply understand the work of Christ. That's an important reminder, especially for those of us who spend our days mostly in
conversation with others within our theological circles.

Sometimes we need a reminder to turn the cross around.

LITERALLY

That said, this emphasis on unity cannot equal silence or complicity. If, as I argued in chapter six, we must be people who speak out against wrongs and work against the justification of broken systems, then we must also be a community for whom the right use of language matters. We must be people from whom a stewardly responsibility exists toward "whatever is true, whatever is noble, whatever is right, whatever is pure, whatever is lovely, whatever is admirable" (Phil 4:8).

It's why I was struck by the report of former White House chief of staff Mick Mulvaney's remark on *Meet the Press* in the waning days of the Trump administration: "People took him literally. I never thought I'd see that."[4] The surprise that is evinced in the statement, "People took him literally." As if to say, "we all know that politicians don't mean what they say. We all know this is a game, an abstraction, a cynical exercise of power. Even if the lies have been escalating in recent months, even if conspiracy theories have been wildly encouraged, even if no evidence exists—why, we've been saying stuff like this for years. Surely no one would actually believe it. C'mon, it's a game." It says a lot about this Age of Irony—where nothing is in earnest—and about a political system where rhetoric is so often detached from reality. It's an irresponsible and cynical way of thinking that has permeated a lot of our discourse, regardless of political party.

Except, it turns out, words do matter. Stories (including the most ludicrous and seemingly unbelievable of conspiracy theories) do have incredible power. Particularly when they are repeated again and again over years and years. People are persuaded. The way we use words, the stories we tell are ways we disciple our minds—and the consequences when we misuse them are very real. Language may have no materiality, but that does not mean that it has no

material effect. The consequences, in fact, put me in mind of one
of Wendell Berry's Sabbath poems, when he says, "A mind that has
confronted ruin for years / Is half or more a ruined mind."[5] Berry's
point: more than the mind is "ruined" by the narrative of devastation and destruction. Everything is disfigured and uglified by it.

It feels like I am stating the obvious: words are more powerful
than sticks and stones. But do we act like it? And perhaps more
importantly, what are the things we *are* willing to admit we take
literally ourselves? Is there anything? Or are we creatures of abstraction, too sophisticated to be in earnest about anything or too
timid to admit it? So much of what seems to pass for Christianity
these days often appears as performative abstraction, cultural allegiance, a social club. Our faith commitments can seem as hollow
(and as self-interested) as our political ones. Surely no one really
believes that anything we say *really* matters. Isn't vague assent to a
checklist of "right" thinking (however that may be defined in one's
theological or political camp) enough? Or is it possible to say anything at all?

Inadequate, inarticulate, and overwhelmed we may feel. But the
time for embodiment—in word and deed together—is every day,
not just when crisis forces it upon us. The challenge: to ask ourselves, *Would anyone feel surprised if you acted on what you say you
literally believe? Would anyone feel surprised that you acted in a way
that your words haven't indicated?* Whatever the areas are where the
answer is yes, we must commit, God helping us, to begin to bring
right thinking and right action into ever greater accord, joining our
voices with others already bravely speaking out.

This goes another way as well: into resisting the impulse to
censor, something that requires vigilance in an open society. It
seems a timelier reminder than ever—for if recent history tells us
nothing else, it is that the stories we tell ourselves as a culture are

more contested than has been perhaps acknowledged. What does citizenship mean, for example? What does it take to be American? Or un-American? Unpatriotic? What does it mean to be Christian? What narratives have dominated, and in so doing, elided others? How does the way the past is described influence the way we are experiencing the present and anticipating the future?

We all know that every story can sound very different, depending on the narrator. Who is the *I* that is speaking, who is the *we* with which they are participating and with whom they'd like us to sympathize or to reject or to critique or to whatever? What does that perspective lead one toward (and also away from)? It's amazing how much readers automatically identify with and normalize the perspective of a first-person narrator—to the point that mystery writers like Agatha Christie quite famously have employed the technique to literarily get away with murder in their novels. But that's true of our approach to Bible stories too: to decorate your child's nursery with a Noah's Ark motif can only happen if you identify yourself with Noah's family and not the ocean of drowned humanity. We need always be mindful of this interpretive principle: Who's on the boat (and who isn't)? How limited is your reading based on where you're placing yourself in the story?

Even as we need to be attentive to perspective, though, what's striking (and yes, for me, depressing) is how often professed Christians have led the charge to limit the narrative, to tell less of the story. Whether that's actually banning texts or advocating to limit parts of history that are perceived as unflattering or uncomfortable, there is a pernicious urge among some Christians to move not toward a gospel plenitude but toward ever smaller explanations, toward a grim "rightness." Discomfort, too, should signal to us something that needs to be faced, not something to flee from. If the Holy Spirit is at work in our imaginative lives, then stories that rattle us are tools to move us toward self-examination, repentance, and reconciliation.

Because we are desperate for more stories, not fewer. Stories that ask the reader, as Flannery O'Connor urged, to get a little dirty when they engage the world as it really is. That includes all the desolation of a broken world but also the deep assurance of the God who redeems it all. I love the way Katherine Paterson—herself a person of robust faith but also someone whose books featured on the top ten banned books list for many years—puts it:

> If knowledge without a sense of reverence is dangerous, morality divorced from wonder leads either to chilling legalism or priggish sentimentality. I am always nervous when some well-meaning critic applauds my work for the values and lessons it teaches children, and I'm almost rude when someone asks me what moral I am trying to teach in a given book. When I write a book I am not setting out to teach virtue, I am trying to tell a story, I am trying to draw my reader into the mystery of human life in this world. I am trying to share my own sense of wonder that although I have not always been in this world and will not continue in it for too many more years, I am here now, sharing in the mystery of the universe, thinking, feeling, tasting, smelling, seeing, hearing, shouting, singing, speaking, laughing, crying, living, and dying.[6]

Our witness demands no less. Only a small god demands an ever-shrinking story.

UNITY AND STABILITY

When we demand an ever-shrinking story, it is because so often *community* is just a cover, a code word, for boundary keeping. Deciding who is in and who is out, who belongs in our *we*. In these contexts, community doesn't mean welcome and inclusion, it means finding the shibboleths to keep people out. As one of my favorite hymns, "There's a Wideness in God's Mercy," puts it,

But we make God's love too narrow
by false limits of our own,
and we magnify its strictness
with a zeal God will not own.[7]

How might we work against that tendency? When Kathleen Norris gave the Buechner Institute's annual lectureship, I was taken by the answer she gave when asked to discuss the vows she had made when she joined a community as an oblate of the Benedictine monastery Assumption Abbey. In her response Norris emphasized that Benedictines take two vows: the vow of stability and the vow of conversion. With the first, Benedictines promise to remain with the same community in the same place for the rest of their lives. I had not realized that Benedictines commit not just to an order but to a very specific iteration of that order. In other words, the monastery they enter will be the one they are in when they are buried. As someone who has moved frequently, I marveled at the testimony of people willing to make such a vow. For all our much-vaunted talk about community, I wonder if (or how much) we are really willing to put in the hard work required to achieve community, even in small measure. Outside monastic orders, has the church lost the ability to nurture this at least in some form? Do we care if we can't—or is it all too much bother anyway?

At the same time, Norris noted, the vow of stability is importantly counterweighted by the vow of conversion. As Norris explained it, this is a promise to continue to grow and develop as a person of faith; it is a vow that values change. Thus, the vow of stability alone could lead to stagnation ("we're rooted here, and it needs to stay like it always has"), while the vow of conversion could lead to valuing change above all, but taken together, they provide a compelling model.

But it seems important that we pursue such a model without an accompanying nostalgia—which also seems to frequently feature in stories of community. As a literature professor, I know that home is a very powerful concept for many writers—who return, again and again, to celebrate and explore the landscapes of their youth. I have friends, too, who speak powerfully of the draw of their "home place," friends who—wherever else they live and for however long—never feel at ease, but Odysseus-like always struggle to return, even if it is only in retirement or the occasional trip back "home." Most of the people I know who grew up rooted in a place are convinced that their particular spot is God's habitation, more winsome than anywhere else.

To be honest, I understand the metaphor intellectually, but it doesn't really connect for me. In fact, I imagine these sentiments stick out to me because my experience is exactly the opposite from what they insist on. I can't give a very concise answer to the question "Where are you from?": before I graduated from high school, I had moved nine times and lived in twelve different houses in three different countries. I have no childhood home to be nostalgic for. My formative landscapes are prairies *and* mountains, high deserts *and* oceans, Asian cities *and* American farmland. Landscape doesn't matter to me—or rather, I find all manner of places beautiful, even if I don't feel I belong to any one of them.

As a child, I remember wondering what it would be like to have only lived in one place with your extended family nearby; as a teenager, I wondered what it would be like to have lifelong friends, people you'd known since kindergarten or before, instead of being the new girl every couple of years. But these musings were more curiosity than envy—after all, who would want to be stuck in one place when the world was on offer? As Elizabeth Bishop asks in "Questions of Travel," "Should we have stayed at home / wherever that may be?"[8] To my mind, the answer was clearly no.

But as I noted above, the definitive word to consider is *we*. I didn't mind moving, because home depended not on place but on people. My immediate family, of course, but perhaps just as importantly, my bigger *we*: our church family. No matter where we lived, our family's life revolved around church and our fellowship there. Every time we moved, my parents spoke confidently about God's call to the next duty station and modeled great trust that, in the words of Julian of Norwich, "all shall be well and all shall be well."[9] And it was: every new place brought fresh evidence of God's providential care for us, new ways to discover the abundance of God's goodness through his creation—but especially through his people. It's notable, I think, how often the Bible tells stories of people asked to leave their homes in order to more fully follow God. One could almost argue that it's a necessity to help develop their full dependence upon God. Abraham, Moses and the Israelites, Ruth: just a few examples of folks who in leaving home find their true home, indeed.

It's notable, too, (as I argued in chapter 4) how Jesus reformulates the family into the brothers and sisters, not of blood, but of shared belief. In so doing, he relocates home from a physical location to one built of living stones. All of this should give us a more capacious definition of where we're from and the community to which we belong. And perhaps it will help us hear anew the verses throughout Scripture that place the welcome of the stranger at the center of what it means to live a Christian life. Too often, I think, we read those words from the perspective of the host—but what might happen if we read them with the understanding that we are the strangers?

But even if *home* is a useful metaphor, perhaps we need to rethink and refine it to reflect the values we say we have about community.

MAKING ROOM

I share a birthday with Virginia Woolf, so perhaps it's not surprising that possibly the best birthday present I've ever received was a room of my own. For much of my childhood, I shared a bedroom with my younger sister, Jane. Five years and eight months different in age, my much younger sister. We got along just fine, however, even if Jane's doll collection of Strawberry Shortcake and her many odiferous friends sometimes took over most of our floor space. I usually wanted to read anyway. Generally, we lived on Army posts in quarters—but for one stretch, we owned a house off-base: a modest three-bedroom 1970s ranch. It certainly never occurred to me to think about having my own room there. From whence would such a thing materialize? So I never asked for one. But as I approached my twelfth birthday, my parents thought I might like to have a space of my own. They wanted to find a way give me some privacy and independence as I moved into adolescence.

They told me they wanted to give me my own room for my birthday. And that's how the breakfast nook in the kitchen became my bedroom.

Looking back, it was smaller than many jail cells, but it gave me tremendous freedom and joy. The width of the room was the width of my twin bed—which fit perfectly under the window between the refrigerator and the wall. I was super excited (as only a child of the '70s can be) that my parents let me hang a silvery metallic butterfly poster on the side of the refrigerator at the foot of the bed. I selected a mustard yellow pillow chair for the other end and was given a lap desk so I could do my homework, luxury of luxuries, sitting on the bed (this in a house where sitting on the bed was firmly discouraged). My mother made new curtains for the room and then used the same fabric to cover a wooden screen that formed the "wall" between my bedroom and the kitchen. In front of the screen stood a small green metal bookshelf that held my record player and books. On the opposite wall, my parents bought a large wooden combination closet and chest of drawers to house my clothes. And on the wall across from the bed was a tiny wicker love seat. I could stand in the middle and touch everything in the room.

And I could not have loved it more.

As I look back on it as an adult, I'm struck by the effort my parents made to make it all happen. Not just the work to make my room—but more importantly, how that one decision meant that the whole house got rearranged, too. For example, the door that used to lead from the kitchen through the breakfast nook to the dining room was now blocked by my bedroom "wall," so the old family room became the new dining room and vice versa. My parents did not speak of their inconvenience—perhaps because it ultimately wasn't for them. Instead, to live well in a home with others is to think about the flourishing of everyone in the household, lovingly rearranging ourselves to find spaces for all. In the household of God, no one is a guest or a visitor. And when someone is made to feel that they are, it is an indicator that we are not yet the community we strive to be.

SMALL STEPS AT GREAT COST

The Tracy K. Smith poem that opens this chapter concludes by narrating how the world begins to heal: by acknowledging the impermanence of human efforts ("When at last we knew how little / Would survive us") and the collective inability of selfish desires to be constructive ("how little we had mended / Or built that was not now lost"). Then the epiphany happens: "something / Large and old awoke." The poem ends with these lines:

>   And then our singing
> Brought on a different manner of weather.
> Then animals long believed gone crept down
> From trees. We took new stock of one another.
> We wept to be reminded of such color.

It's instructive to see that it is the move to "singing"—in other words, a creative response—that changes the atmosphere, that allows previously disappeared creatures to return. But best of all, an acknowledgment of human limitations allows the people in the poem to see each other anew, reveling now in the diversity that previously separated them.

It's a beautiful vision. And, if anything, we need to consider how to shape our song, so that we move to the end of the poem, instead of remaining mired in the reality that the poem's opening details. Certainly, I've already suggested several principles in this chapter to help us move to a better envisioning of community, but let me conclude with a final one: being attentive to what language most attracts us when we talk about community.

A few years ago I watched a BBC2 import on Netflix called *Churchill's Secret Agents: The New Recruits*. It chronicled the story of the Special Operations Executive (SOE), a secret group, set up just as World War II was starting, for clandestine work: spying, helping the resistance, carrying out missions to demolish various critical infrastructure (roads, bridges, depots, etc.), and establishing communication networks. Significantly, both men and women served—people from all walks of life. And these ordinary folks, dropped perilously behind enemy lines, were then involved in some of the war's most dangerous missions—from the destruction of Norway's heavy water plant to Czechoslovakia's Operation Anthropoid, the assassination of a high-ranking Nazi official.

Their survival rate was incredibly low, so training was essential. And this is where the "new recruits" part of the show comes in. Rather than simply narrate the history of the SOE and its many missions, the documentary decides to show just what it took to become members of the SOE (or for Americans, the OSS) by cleverly weaving in that history—and the individual stories of SOE officers—with an immersive "living history" experiment. We follow, then, fourteen participants who gather in the remote Scottish Highlands to go through intense training that replicates the original 1940s SOE syllabus. They do everything to period (including dress and food) and are put through their very difficult paces and evaluated by currently serving British military officers. Just as in the 1940s, the participants don't all make it through—the rigor of the training is not minimized. But the documentary insists, particularly by connecting the modern-day participants with historical ones, that past heroes were not nine feet tall—and these participants needn't be, either.

Most importantly, the series is clear: it took many people, doing small missions everywhere, to make a difference. The program's point: we never defeat evil alone but only in small steps and at very great cost. Significantly, the program was not about who "wins" the competition: indeed, it was not set up to have a winner. The last episode of the series shows the participants who have completed the training work together to achieve one complex assignment together.

And here's the language they used as they worked toward successfully accomplishing their goal: the language of self-sacrifice, of duty, of team. Of thinking about what was good for all, rather than convenient for some. Of planning for team members' strengths and weaknesses, instead of dismissing or disregarding them. Such language stood out to me because it was such a contrast to what we heard in so many places during Covid: the language of "rights."

One of the ways that has manifested itself is resistance to public health measures, like mask wearing. I have to admit that I'm rather perplexed at how it became such a hot topic. Part of my childhood was spent in Korea and Japan where masks are common whenever a person feels ill. It's simply courteous—and it's very common to see masked people, for example, on public transportation. Admittedly, there was mixed messaging about mask wearing very early on (and certainly, I understand that exceptions are necessary). But overall, the amount of adult fit-throwing in Costco and Trader Joe's stores across the nation, captured on social media, is rather mind-blowing.

What gets repeated most in these objections is that such requirements are an infringement of "rights." That "living in a free country" means one needn't "be a sheep." What's curious in their concept of law and community is that these folks *do* seem willing to obey the shirts and shoes rules of these same stores but find the restrictions of a mask ovine. They also insist that private businesses should have all kinds of latitude about what kinds of rules they can make to *not* serve certain customers by refusing to bake cakes or take photographs or whatever—but they seem to not believe that those businesses have the same rights to make rules that apply to *them*.

As confounding as this all is, I actually think this is not the issue we should debate. To engage it is not to engage the more central question. Instead, I believe that if we are Christians, we go down an unproductive road when we default to the language of rights. As Americans, we love to talk about our rights to all sorts of things—and don't get me wrong, I am grateful for our many freedoms—but I wonder about our witness as people of faith if this is our primary discourse, the main way we frame situations. In fact, I do believe everyone has rights (so there's no argument to be had)—but I don't believe that our rights should have primacy in shaping our responses.

Instead, it has been helpful for me to think about my own response to Covid-19 in light of *kenosis*, the idea of Christ's self-emptying. In Philippians 2, Paul explains this concept:

> Do nothing out of selfish ambition or vain conceit. Rather,
> in humility value others above yourselves, not looking
> to your own interests but each of you to the interests
> of the others.
>
> In your relationships with one another, have the same
> mindset as Christ Jesus:
>
> Who, being in very nature God,
> did not consider equality with God something to be used
> to his own advantage;
>
> rather, he made himself nothing
> by taking the very nature of a servant,
> being made in human likeness.
>
> And being found in appearance as a man,
> he humbled himself
> by becoming obedient to death—
> even death on a cross! (Phil 2:3-8)

In other words, Christ—who had the *right* to absolutely everything, to every "advantage"—gave it all up out of love. In order to serve, even unto death. Paul is clear that as Jesus' followers we must cultivate this "same mindset": even if we have a superior claim, we put others' interests ahead of our own. In this pursuit of humility, then, Christianity is completely at odds with a rights-driven orientation. In other words, it doesn't actually matter if I have the right to do something or not. And even granting that I do, if it is not helping me lovingly and humbly serve the "interest of others," it is not something I should be pursuing. Think about Jesus' command to go the extra mile (even if requested by a hostile colonizing oppressor) or to give one's cloak *and* one's coat or to forgive beyond what is required. The minute my most pressing motivation is "my right," I move away from the kenotic stance that my faith requires of me—and I move away from the direct command of Jesus. When I'm attracted to the language of "rights," I get alerted to my own motivations.

Our faithful witness in the world doesn't end in times of crisis—in fact, these times magnify our real beliefs through the actions and attitudes we adopt. Communities reveal themselves in crisis. Teaching throughout the pandemic has showed me what could happen when people prioritized each other. Through it all, I was struck by how much students wanted to be together, wanted to participate, wanted to do their best. And they did. Much of the success was also down to an administrative team who planned carefully, a staff who delivered IT help and disinfected buildings and coordinated student care in the residence halls and so much more, and a faculty who collaborated with each other to solve technological and pedagogical challenges. Was it always perfect? No, but every community is always in process, striving to live together imperfectly.

We need to remember our essentials: it's not "political" to care about others. We can vote however we feel led, and we can work for the protections promised to all our citizens. But like Christians across the centuries, we should be marked by our radical care for others, even when we don't "have to," even when we have a right not to.

After all, it's okay to be in a community of sheep if you're following the Lamb.

8

Root-Room

Soul, self; come, poor Jackself, I do advise
You, jaded, let be; call off thoughts awhile
Elsewhere; leave comfort root-room; let joy size
At God knows when to God knows what.

GERARD MANLEY HOPKINS,
"MY OWN HEART LET ME MORE HAVE PITY ON"

WHAT ALL THE PROCEEDING CHAPTERS have been leading toward is this: to bring together the necessary components to ultimately tell a story of hope. Certainly, Christians should be people who both embrace nuance and fully acknowledge the difficult complexities of every human story. And yet, even with those caveats, we can also affirm that the stories we tell are comedies, not tragedies, in the classical sense that comedies end with a move toward life and restoration. Death, as Frederick Buechner has observed, is only the penultimate word—never the final one.[1] Our stories as people of faith, then, are always tinged with anticipation, even if sometimes it's only the subtlest acknowledgment of something bigger and more mysterious taking place beyond the limits of our narratives. Knowing our story's ultimate end should help us live into grace more fully.

This push toward narrative hope is something that the Bible itself models for us. Isn't it interesting that Scripture doesn't erase all the bad things that happened? One could imagine a religious text that might find it easier to simply give rules or assert spiritual abstractions. Wouldn't it have been easier to not give a report of all the times the Israelites were disobedient? Mightn't it have been more effective to have a New Testament full of clear rules, rather than assemble a collection of letters that chronicle all the dysfunctions of the early church? As a mental exercise, imagining a different construction of the Bible highlights the fact that the Bible doesn't shy away from the hard stuff—instead, it's almost exclusively the hard stuff. Except that the hard stuff doesn't get to win.

I am struck, for example, by how many verses about floods and storms are contained in Scripture. Whether natural or metaphorical, it is clear that few things expose our feeble power, our incredible fantasies of control, more than raging water, whatever form it takes. Like in the magnificent short Psalm 93, full of overwhelming deluges. After establishing God's regality, the poem moves to the might of the rushing waters:

> The LORD reigns, He is clothed with majesty;
> The LORD has clothed and girded Himself with strength;
> Indeed, the world is firmly established, it will not be moved.
> Your throne is established from of old;
> You are from everlasting.
>
> The floods have lifted up, O LORD,
> The floods have lifted up their voice,
> The floods lift up their pounding waves.
> More than the sounds of many waters,
> Than the mighty breakers of the sea,
> The LORD on high is mighty.

Your testimonies are fully confirmed;
Holiness befits Your house,
O LORD, forevermore. (Ps 93:1-5 NASB 1995)

The middle of the poem evokes calamity—and yet, as John Calvin
reflects in his commentary on this psalm, "it is then declared that
such is [God's] faithfulness that he never deceives his own people,
who, embracing his promises, wait with tranquil minds for their
salvation amidst all the tempests and agitations of the world."[2] Think
about that: Calvin's sense that part of God's faithfulness is his recognition of the destructive mightiness of the floods. There is no diminishment of the real terror of the loud and looming waters, but these
"tempests and agitations of the world" (what a wonderful phrase!)
can be borne and put into context because God's stories ("your testimonies") about God's greater power are "fully confirmed." This is
the balance the Christian story celebrates. Our faith does not require that we deny the existence of the thundering voices of the
floods; it simply asks us to know that there is a louder voice still.

C. S. Lewis in his marvelous essay "Learning in War-Time"
(written during World War II) makes a similar point:

> The war creates no absolutely new situation: it simply aggra-
> vates the permanent human situation so that we can no longer
> ignore it. Human life has always been lived on the edge of a
> precipice. Human culture has always had to exist under the
> shadow of something infinitely more important than itself. If
> men had postponed the search for knowledge and beauty
> until they were secure, the search would never have begun.
> We are mistaken when we compare war with "normal life."
> Life has never been normal.[3]

"Human life has always been lived on the edge of a precipice." Here,
Lewis envisions a house perched on a cliff or a journey traveled

along the treacherous edge—but it's not dangerous because of the
existence of war; the fact is, Lewis asserts, that life is always perilous.
But the danger of life on a precipice cannot negate the search for
wisdom, nor is it an impediment to discovering beauty. And Lewis
rejects the notion that valuable work lies only in the most immediate, the most practical of work (in this context, fighting on the
battlefield). We may be perpetually, as Matthew Arnold observed,
on a "darkling plain [s]wept with confused alarms of struggle and
flight, [w]here ignorant armies clash by night."[4] But Lewis reminds
us that such has it ever been—the idea of "normal life" is a deception.

After the attack at the offices of the satirical French magazine
Charlie Hebdo in Paris in 2015, a provocative image began circu-
lating online. At the top of the picture (under the heading "yesterday") was a long sharpened red pencil. In the middle of the
image (under the heading "today"), the pencil had been broken in
half. But in the bottom image (under the heading "tomorrow"),
both halves of the broken pencil were now sharpened. Originally
attributed to the underground artist Banksy, the art really belonged
to a London illustrator, Lucille Clerc. Clerc's piece resonates, I
think, because of its powerful message of hope: in being broken the
pencil isn't destroyed at all; rather, one pencil has now become
two—doubling the "voice" of the pencil rather than obliterating it.

Or I'm profoundly moved by another visual metaphor, another
powerful artistic response to brokenness: the Japanese art of
kintsugi. *Kintsugi*—which literally means "joined with gold"—is
exactly that: a technique of restoration. But with an important
difference: a shattered piece of pottery (a bowl, a teacup, a plate)
is not discarded, but instead an artisan mends it back together.
Rather than conceal the work of repair and restore the object to
looking "as good as new," however, the craftsperson does exactly
the opposite and highlights the sites of repair with gold. In so

doing, the artisan not only restores the object to use but actually makes it more valuable and more beautiful than it was in its original form.

In our disposable culture, what a powerful idea: that being damaged, even significantly, does not require discarding. That restoration is not only possible but that the broken is more lovely than the perfect. That the signs of repair are not marks of failure to be hidden but marks of witness to enable celebration to the one who repairs us—and with the most precious materials.

MESSED UP MARBLE

Our stories of hope, though, mean nothing if they do not reorient the stories we tell ourselves *about* ourselves. If our stories do not make us gracious to our own self-conceptions. Here I turn a final time to my frequent companion in this book, Gerard Manley Hopkins. Hopkins struggled mightily. After a very successful period as a star student, his conversion to Catholicism at the end of his university career, coupled with his decision to seek ordination as a Jesuit priest, derailed his plans to have an academic career at Oxbridge. It also deeply upset his family. And his years as a priest were often filled with disappointment and illness.

Toward the end of his life, he wrote a series of poems usually referred to as the "Terrible Sonnets" because they are so brutally honest in their examination of depression and spiritual alienation. Hopkins excoriates himself and his many failings, real and perceived. He chronicles the precarity of mental illness. He cries out for an absent God. But toward the end of the sonnet cycle, Hopkins composed the line "My own heart let me more have pity on" that begins to recognize where hope may be found. First, though, the poem opens desiring an escape from his "tormented mind tormenting yet." Note the circularity of the language in stanza one:

My own heart let me more have pity on; let
Me live to my sad self hereafter kind,
Charitable; not live this tormented mind
With this tormented mind tormenting yet.
I cast for comfort I can no more get
By groping round my comfortless, than blind
Eyes in their dark can day or thirst can find
Thirst's all-in-all in all a world of wet.[5]

Hopkins recognizes that it is incredibly difficult to rescue oneself during one's own suffering. Instead, the poem's opening self-advice (I need to have more pity on myself, be kinder to myself) helps him begin to rethink his narrative so that he can find ways to get out of the circles and cycles of self-judgment and extend self-kindness, even in his darkest moments.

The second stanza, then, offers what may look like simple advice:

Soul, self; come, poor Jackself, I do advise
You, jaded, let be; call off thoughts awhile
Elsewhere; leave comfort root-room; let joy size
At God knows when to God knows what; whose smile
's not wrung, see you; unforeseen times rather — as skies
Betweenpie mountains — lights a lovely mile.

But I'm not sure it is so simple. The poem argues that what *can* be done is trying to reframe one's outlook, rejecting self-conscious "jaded-ness." To find joy in the unexpected, like the way that light peeks between the mountains. God's smile isn't predictable, but it shows up in unexpected times and places illuminating our way. And the key line: "leave comfort root-room." In other words, make sure to give space for consolation to take hold in your life. For hope to grow in a life, it needs to be intentionally cultivated.

Another part of Hopkins's struggle is his conception of himself—in "My own heart" he poignantly names his pain and even begins to move toward strategies for healing. But since it does not really resolve his sense of his own internal wretchedness, we need, perhaps, one more example to think hopefully about our own failings.

When I take students studying Dante's *Divine Comedy* to Florence, we visit Michelangelo's *David* in the Accademia. Replicated everywhere one looks—from expected items like small plaster statues and T-shirts to the trashy "crotch shot," which adorns underwear and aprons displayed in front of tourist shops— the *David* is nevertheless one tourist attraction that does not disappoint. Situated under a beautifully lit dome located majestically at the end of a long gallery, the David is breathtaking in its grandeur and in its celebration of the human form. Everyone in my group was wowed by the scale of the artistry.

And yet, our guide Anna focused on the many "imperfections" of the *David*: the too-big hand, the imperfections in the proportions of the body, the overly large head, the tree stump behind one of David's legs. She talked about all the ways the statue shouldn't actually work.

But maybe more importantly, she told us about why some of these "imperfections" exist. It turns out that Michelangelo wasn't the first sculptor commissioned to undertake the *David*. Instead, the folks in charge of the Duomo, Florence's cathedral, contracted a guy named Agostino di Duccio in 1464. He was supposed to make the statue as one of a series of pieces that would go into alcoves around the church, high above the ground. For two years, di Duccio hacked away at the enormous piece of Carrara marble the city had procured for the project. But he didn't finish—and he claimed the marble wasn't very good. A decade later, another guy, Antonio Rossellino, was given a whack. And although his contract was terminated quickly, he too complained about the quality of the marble.

For the next twenty-five years, then, the disfigured piece of marble stood outside. When in 1501 the twenty-six-year-old Michelangelo set to work on one of his very first commissions, he started with some pretty serious problems. An inventory of the Duomo's holdings described the piece as "a certain figure of marble called David, badly blocked out and supine."[6]

How could Michelangelo create something when the starting materials were so badly damaged by the incompetence of others? Why bother? For two years, Michelangelo labored in secret to create his David, including adding that tree stump to give di Duccio's badly begun leg sufficient support. A David different from other Renaissance renderings in that his David stands steel-eyed and ready, right before his battle with Goliath—as opposed to so many other statues of David that feature him post-battle, with Goliath's head under his foot.

As I heard this story of the inauspicious beginning of one of the world's acknowledged masterpieces, I felt enormously hopeful. How encouraging to think that with the right artist at work in our lives, our bad beginnings—even the wounding, seemingly disfiguring "cuts" made by circumstances and by other people—aren't the last word. And that even neglected for many years, something beautiful can always still emerge. Even wrecked materials are no obstacle to the Creator of the universe.

THE SLIGHTEST HINT OF GREEN

An orientation toward hope changes our stories about ourselves, and it should make us gracious to the wounds and failings of the church as well.

I've nicknamed my general education global literature class "Epic Journeys." That means we read lots of long stuff from the ancient and medieval world characterized by people on the move: *Gilgamesh, The Odyssey, The Aeneid, The Voyages of Sinbad, Laxdaela Saga,* and my beloved *Divine Comedy.* Of course, *journey* is a wellworn conceit—but even so, that doesn't mean that these texts still don't yield rich questions to consider. Nothing survives as long as these books have unless it continues to compel us: Why is the protagonist on the road? What challenges stand in the way of the journey's end—and how are they handled? What do the characteristics of the protagonist tell us about the values of a given society? What is the role of the divine?

And then there's one that I found particularly compelling the last time I taught the course: What is to be learned from the people encountered along the way?

In the *Divine Comedy,* the answer is particularly profound. Unlike all the other epic heroes, Dante can't make it alone—importantly, he has multiple guides on his trip through hell, purgatory, and paradise. Unlike wily Odysseus and dutiful Aeneas, Dante the Pilgrim is fearful and timid and full of questions. In fact, as he travels and meets person after person, his almost constant refrain (including in the beginning cantos of *Paradiso* itself) is "what are you doing here?" The implication is that Dante the Pilgrim is astonished because he has clearly made assumptions about the eternal destinies of people he knew, either personally or by reputation. Nevertheless, Dante the Pilgrim's question forces the reader to ask the same question: Why are we surprised? Why do we often agree with Dante when he questions people's placement? What assumptions do we make about who is saved and who is not? About where they are and its fairness? The poem's answer seems to be that we need to figure out only our own journey. Everyone else is not our business.

This lesson is particularly evident in canto III of *Purgatorio*. Dante comes across Manfred, a great warrior and leader, who was famously excommunicated by the pope and buried in unhallowed ground. Yet here he is in purgatory, repenting of his sins and being sanctified for his final destination in paradise. Dante is amazed but Manfred explains:

> Horrible was the nature of my sins,
> But boundless mercy stretches out its arms
> To any man who comes in search of it . . .
> The church's curse is not the final word,
> for Everlasting Love may still return,
> if hope reveals the slightest hint of green.[7]

Note the powerful assertion: "The church's curse is not the final word." Only "Everlasting Love" gets to make the final determination. Manfred testifies to the reality that nothing can separate us from the love of God—nothing that we can do. But certainly, no human beings, even religious leaders, get that authority.

When my students wrote in their final exams about reading the *Divine Comedy*, many returned to this passage as a place of hope for them. In a time when social media is constantly filled with stories of churches who wound and reject, in a time when church might feel increasingly irrelevant, my students wrestle with the place of the church in their own lives. What does it mean to be part of increasingly fraught denominations these days? How do we accomplish that "long obedience in the same direction"?[8] Dante's own long journey gives us one epic answer: love and support the *right* workings of the church (the subject of much of *Paradiso*), but remember that the aim of the journey is knowing God—the God who pursues us even into hell, saves us despite what anyone else might think, and points our vision upward to the "Love that moves the sun and the other stars."[9] Only that God gets the last word.

WALKING AND LEAPING

These are all important narratives of hope, but the genre, perhaps, that can most attune us to hope is stories of healing.

It was my turn to be the storyteller for the elementary-school-age kids during Sunday school. According to our material, our theme for the month was *determination*, and our text that day was Acts 3–4, where John and Peter, in the midst of proclaiming the gospel, heal a crippled man at the Beautiful Gate and then face the wrath (including a stint in prison) of the Sanhedrin. The point of the lesson, then, was supposed to be how the apostles kept going even as they faced opposition at every turn.

Well sure, true enough. But ever since I broke my foot and was unable to walk or drive for months, I've become especially attuned to the many times *lameness* is spoken of in the Bible. Turns out it's all over hymns too. But just like we rather blithely use other kinds of disability language (blindness and deafness are two other big ones), our discussions of lameness far too often reduce the lived experience of a person into an abstraction. So before we got to Peter and John and the Sanhedrin, the kids and I wondered together about the man at the Beautiful Gate. What would it have been like for *him*? What kind of determination had *he* needed to go there every day and to ask for money, particularly since he would have been unable to have any other kind of employment? What else would he have liked to do with his life? What was it like to sit there every day, to have to depend on friends and family to bring him anywhere he wanted to go? We talked, too, about the fact that the text suggests that until John and Peter look at him, he isn't accustomed to being really seen for himself—or not being dismissed as anything more than a beggar.

I shared with the kids what it had been like for me to not walk for only a short period of time compared to this man—and of all the adjustments I was forced to make, of all the things that were hard (including getting around inside our very church building), of all the things I ended up not being able to do at all. But also about how extraordinarily happy I was the day I was told I could finally drive again. "Walking and leaping and praising God," indeed.

And in fact, it is the man's irrepressible joy as witnessed by all the folks around the Temple—the embodied miracle of his very life—that demands an accounting. As Denise Levertov puts it in her poem "On Belief in the Physical Resurrection of Jesus," metaphor and sign, beautiful as they are, don't work unless they are grounded in reality—and in a God who loves us, body *and* soul.[10]

But it's not just the fact of God's total love for us in a very embodied way, it is that the healing itself is very personalized. Another story I got to tell the kids another Sunday was about Jesus' healing of the blind man at the pool of Siloam (John 9). This is the one where Jesus uses mud he made by spitting in dirt and applies it to the eyes of a man who has been blind his entire life. Restoration of sight and lots of fun interactions with the Pharisees follow.

For me the mud-making, eye-smearing aspect was what got my attention. We know from other parts of the Gospels that Jesus can heal with a word: Why go to this messy trouble? Surveying all the ways Jesus heals in Scripture raises yet another question. First, just a reminder of a few of those ways:

- By question ("Do you want to be healed?"), followed by direct command in John 5
- By touching the leper in Matthew 8
- By distant command for the centurion's servant in Luke 7
- By Jesus being touched by someone and he assents (like the woman "subject to bleeding"), Matthew 9
- By assertion (all over the place)

Even in this small sample of healing, it seems like there might be at least two related things going on: (1) a truly personal God who takes time to particularize our healing because (2) the method of healing has meaning too. This is no generic chanting of the same words (not that there'd be anything wrong with that, had Jesus chosen that). But how much more powerful to realize that people receive healing in ways that are meaningful to them. So a touchless word to the leper would have reinforced his untouchableness, while being touched is an affirmation of the man's wholeness. The centurion operates in a world where command to unseen folks is a sign of authority—Jesus doesn't need to go to the centurion's servant because that's not needed by the truly powerful. The means are ministry.

And for the blind man and his mud-pie treatment: the Bible is clear that he was born blind, so that the tactile would have been an important way of knowing for him. In some ways, maybe the application of the mud on his eyes let him participate too—that is, to feel the mud was a more profound way of experiencing his healing than through the abstraction of words.

Yet when we look for hope, don't we often act like we think healing will look the same for everyone? Maybe we're missing some moments of restoration by expecting the cookie-cutter approach. At the very least, it feels like a kind of grace to have glimpses of the lengths God goes—the divine particularity of participation—to redeem our messy lives. And the lengths are great, indeed. For Lent one year, I read an illustrated devotional on the book of Mark assembled by a friend's church. One drawing really stuck out to me. A pencil drawing, startling in its simplicity, depicted the story of the woman with the so-called issue of blood from Mark 5. In this story, this woman had "been subject to bleeding for twelve years" and had spent all her money on doctors who had only made her worse (Mk 5:25-26). She believed if she could only touch Jesus' clothes, she would be healed. In this depiction, Jesus is in the foreground, surrounded by children who hold his hand, cling to his neck, and joyfully lope alongside him as he walks. All around, large, dark robe shapes signifying the thronging masses loom. And to the left side, the woman herself is portrayed. Significantly, she is depicted in the same light tones as Jesus, not in the dark garments of the crowd. Here we see her kneeling on the ground, leaning slightly forward at just the moment before she touches Jesus. In her gesture, you can detect both her tentativeness and her tenacity.

Her tentativeness and tenacity are both understandable when we remember the Levitical prohibitions she was up against. Many scholars believe she was suffering from what is medically termed menorrhagia (or abnormally heavy menstruation that is not only painful and messy but can cause profound anemia and make everyday activities difficult). The Law said that if a woman's period lasted beyond seven days (quite normal in sufferers of menorrhagia) she would be unclean all the time, unable to participate in even the most basic things of life, including preparing meals. On top of it, she'd undergone quack treatments that had taken her money and hampered her health. And relationships were impossible: some writers have argued that, if married, the woman's husband might have had to divorce her because being in contact with her would contaminate the entire household. Indeed, anyone who touched her, including all the people in the crowd that day, would themselves become unclean. What she must have been suffering to decide to risk venturing out that day!

The story of the bleeding woman has become an important one to me because I myself developed an "issue of blood" because of uterine fibroids (one of the causes of menorrhagia) that ultimately resulted in a hysterectomy. This admission sometimes makes folks uncomfortable, and I would argue that their discomfort is because women's health issues remain almost as taboo as in earlier times. The stigma surrounding an event that happens to half the population each month remains so strongly in place that, in response, "menstrual equity" is beginning to emerge in policy discussions in areas ranging from taxes, prisons, and manufacturing centers.

But if we've hardly made progress on this issue, Jesus is radically different. In fact, all of Mark 5 is inspiring in its proclamation that there is nothing unmentionable, there is no one untouchable: not the legion-of-demons-possessed man in the first part of the chapter, not this bleeding woman, and not the dead young daughter of Jairus, whose story closes out the chapter. There is no one to whom Christ's healing does not extend, no one who is too unclean to be touched, no situation beyond Christ's power.

Instead, in his interaction with the bleeding woman Christ makes all of this explicit. Jostled by the crowds, Jesus asks upon feeling the woman's touch: "Who touched my clothes?" Given the pressing state of the crowds, the disciples laugh. Who *isn't* touching Jesus? But it's telling that Jesus calls the woman out: he doesn't just heal her silently (as he could have).

Of course, she has to respond. She could have taken her healing and gone away, but as Mark reports, "then the woman came and fell at his feet. She knew what had happened to her. She was shaking with fear. But she told him the whole truth" (Mk 5:32-33). Admitting to her unclean state is risky for this woman—Jesus would then be unclean too. She understands that she and the people of her time were keeping the purity laws as an effort of righteousness, and she is mindful of how she might implicate Jesus. But by making her healing public, Jesus shows both his authority over sin and the nonsense of such categories as "clean" and "unclean": not only is he unchanged in any way because of being touched by her, but she is praised for her faith in doing the very thing that could render him unclean—namely, touching him. By acknowledging and naming her faith, he brings her from the margins and establishes her as a heroine of belief. In the picture that so inspired me, the dark robes turn away from Jesus, but by placing the woman in the same color robes as Jesus, the artist is clear that the woman's faith shines bright. And she is not only physically restored, but as importantly, she is restored relationally: in perhaps the most touching moment of the story, Jesus calls this woman—alienated from family and society by the Law—"daughter." Love restores what law rejects.

If Mark 5 tells us anything it's that there really is nothing that can separate us from the love of God. Every person Jesus meets is faced with a seemingly impossible situation, a situation they can do nothing to fix themselves. Yet the tentative hand of a hurting woman, reaching out in faith—even if only to barely brush the surface—seems like a fitting image for all of us who tremblingly seek the Savior.

SOUR-SWEET DAYS

And when healing seems elusive? I think of the late Anya Krugovoy Silver, an extremely gifted poet and an incredible woman of faith. At her death she was only forty-nine, much too young. I only ever got to see her at Calvin University's Festival of Faith & Writing—where we all loved having her both as an attendee and as a presenter—but she was such a person of radiance that each interchange I got to have with her was filled with great delight. I will miss her incandescence.

At the last Festival she attended, one of her sessions was discussing joy with several other poets. I think it is one of the key themes of her poetry—despite, or perhaps because of, her diagnosis while pregnant with her son, Noah, of inflammatory breast cancer, one of the rarest cancers with a bleak five-year survival rate. But it was not a cavalier joy—it was one rooted in an honesty and a truth-telling and an examination of every hard thing. In her second collection of poetry, *The Ninety-Third Name of God: Poems*, she includes an epigraph from George Herbert that could be a credo: "And all my sour-sweet days / I will lament and love."[11]

That balance—sour and sweet, lament and love—shows up brilliantly in all her words. She was clear that she was not reducible to cancer, that it was not the number one thing about her identity. She wanted to narrate the coexistence of cancer and pregnancy, motherhood and mortality, an all-loving God with the relentless trauma of illness and loss. She explained how she navigated this:

> My first faith response to my [diagnosis] was intense anger at God. Of course, this is the old question of theodicy. Why would God allow me to become pregnant and then a mother only to curse me with a terminal disease? . . . I had not been attending church in the few years before my pregnancy, but I now found the need for answers to existential questions that religion brings. The first service that I attended was a baptism. I watched as joyful mothers carried their babies up and down the aisles of the church. Meanwhile, I stood there, bald and afraid for my life. The triumphant tone of the service left me bitter and lonely, and I ran out of the sanctuary and into the bathroom. There, praying for God's presence, I felt a warm presence enfolding and comforting me. And so, rather than in the pews, I felt God's healing on the floor of the church bathroom. And really, that's not surprising, because that's probably where Jesus would be, wandering the halls of the church, looking for those who, for whatever reason, exclude themselves from the ritual, and lovingly bring them back in. My experience with mothering, therefore, has always been

closely linked to the knowledge that I will die. What will happen to my son when I die? Will he be happy again? Will he believe?

Here's what I've learned: God is with me. God is not just watching from above. God will not decide whether I live or die by how often I pray. God is with me the most when I am at my most lonely and afraid. God will be there for my son. When I call for help, I feel God's presence in calm and peace. As God tells the reader in Isaiah 45:7 (KJV): "I form the light, and create darkness: I make peace, and create evil: I the Lord do all these things." I interpret these enigmatic words not to mean that God literally created and gave me my cancer, but that God is in all things, both the light and darkness, the peace and the evil. Where evil exists, God does not absent God-self. Three simple words: God is there.[12]

"Three simple words: God is there." A breathtaking statement of both challenge and comfort.

Though living through my broken foot is much less consequential than Silver's experience, it did provide insight in its smaller way. It's certainly true that I was thrilled to be able to walk again after my surgery—it felt like a miracle, given how shattered my foot was. But it was never without pain. A couple of years in, I went to physical therapy—which helped some—but not completely.

To be honest, I didn't expect zero pain. As broken as my foot had been, I wanted to be realistic about the limits of healing, and of course, I knew my foot would never be quite the same ever again. I also was well aware of the much more serious chronic pain so many others endure, so it felt self-indulgent to be whiny. Still, as the years passed, it felt like things were getting worse. My doctor had warned me that arthritis might set in—a sort of reverse, malicious *kintsugi*. But this summer as I trooped all over London, walking the city as I've always done each time I have visited, I found I was too hobbled by the end of the day to do anything but hail a cab to get to the hotel. My optimistically purchased Oyster card for the tube went mostly unused because I often felt like I couldn't realistically walk another step.

I finally decided to risk losing my reputation as someone "low maintenance" and ask my doctor about it. She provided me a referral—and I discovered that there were real reasons for my pain, not just the normal condition of a damaged foot. For one thing, the three screws traversing all my metatarsals had become loose (yes, I know—the jokes write themselves here), so they were now hurting, not helping.

My new orthopedic surgeon was wonderful, validating that my pain was real and providing me with a number of treatment options. She explained that part of the pain was also from the undamaged part of my foot bearing too much and, in the process, becoming damaged itself. Years of walking in pain had affected my gait as well and so pain was begetting more pain. Though we're going to pursue a range of options, one of the things she prescribed was a custom orthotic, 3D-printed just for me. The wonder of that little piece of plastic! In the first weeks I had it in my shoe: transformation. It's astonishing what a little support in the right places can do. And it seems like it's important to remind ourselves that so many of us are walking around "healed" but not pain-free, sucking it up so as not to burden anyone. Maybe even dismissing our response because we feel it's probably not significant enough, and accepting the pain is just never going to go away.

And it won't—completely—this side of life. Even so, are we seeking the necessary support to get through it—wherever/ whoever/whatever that might be (and no doubt, in multiple ways)? What spiritual orthotic might help your "walk" improve this year, sustain and undergird those still-weak places, provide relief and joy? How do we tell stories of our pain that don't dismiss it or minimize it, but also include a God who walks beside?

THE LEAP

One thing I've learned: hope is hard. People dismiss it as naive, unsophisticated, un-nuanced. Just plain dumb. How do we find the courage to be hopeful? To articulate the principles we hold and find the courage to carry them out.

Though I was slight and small, I was quite a fearless little kid. When we moved to Korea in the early 1970s, I was six, my brother was four, and my sister was but eight months old. Army housing is assigned by rank and number of children, so our quarters had three bedrooms in one half of a duplex. Given our ages, my parents decided that us kids would have a sleeping room and a playroom— and proceeded to have a bunk bed custom-made for my brother and me. To this day it remains the tallest bunk bed I have ever seen. It dominated the already-small room, a bulwark against all comers and a perfect fort. Against the other wall of the bedroom, perpendicular to the hulking bunk bed, was my sister's crib. Naturally, my brother and I thought it would be great fun to do some precise parachuting from the top of the bunk bed and to launch ourselves into the crib. Looking back, I'm always amazed (a) that we always landed in the crib and not in a heap on the ground with a broken limb or worse, (b) that the crib never broke, and (c) that our mother always discovered us. Perhaps it was the high-pitched shrieking coming from the bedroom that tipped her off.

With a childhood such as that, it will not astonish you to learn that I was probably ten years old or so before I realized I was technically a civilian. So obviously I loved the celebration every year on Armed Forces Day. Since the 1950s, Armed Forces Day has been celebrated on bases around the world, often by opening training facilities to family members and sometimes the general public too.

No surprise, then: that first year in Korea, I decided I wanted to jump out of the parachute training tower. My mother was quite dubious, given how high the tower reached into the sky. It also required that the jumper climb to the top alone—no parent, no nothing.

But despite her protestations, I was determined. And so I began the long climb up. The tower was open on the sides, so you could feel the breeze as you got farther and farther away from the ground. The metal steps were closer to a ladder than a real staircase—and it turns out there were a lot of them.

Midway up, I began to reconsider. I had already climbed a long way, and it seemed like there were still hundreds of steps in front of me. And it was way higher than I had imagined.

Still, looking down, I realized how very scary it would be to climb backward all the way back to the ground. And I knew I couldn't stay paralyzed in the middle of the tower.

I kept climbing.

When I got to the top, the men got me in my harness and told me that because I was so little, I would have to take a running start. Taking off, I whipped down that line so fast that I'm not even sure I was breathing.

Actually, the jump was the least-frightening part of the whole experience because, unlike my solo climb to the top, my father had promised to be at the end of the line, ready to catch me as I landed. In that I had complete confidence. And he did not disappoint.

It's funny, though: when we talked about this recently, he told me he hadn't been too sure, given my velocity, if he would indeed be able to catch me. It's a good thing God is a little stronger, no matter what we throw at him.

Without a story of hope, it's easy to decide to never climb the daunting towers of our lives. It's easy to listen to naysayers, even when they have our good in mind. It's easy to get paralyzed in the middle or think that somehow we can go back to where we were before. It's easy to get weary of the climb.

But thankfully we never climb alone.

In the stories we tell, may we help each other face the arduous climb that lies before each of us, urging each other on to love and good works and reminding ourselves of this truth: that our God goes before us, ready to catch us when we take the leap. That is the essence of hope—and it's an incredibly nourishing narrative to live by.

9

Our Hope for Years to Come

You cannot know . . . what your words
will weigh with students remembering them
in a place you will never see.

Lionel Basney, "Dream of the School"

I BEGAN CHAPTER ONE WITH A STORY about my wonderful fifth grade teacher, Mrs. Ash. Actually, I've been very fortunate in the teachers in my life. Their names come back so easily (many of them assuming almost mythic status in my family's lore): Anquanita Ash, Judy Rogers, Donna Hansen, Lynn Moncus, Darlis Miller, Harriet Linkin. And there were many more. In every one of the eleven schools I attended, teachers took such a strong interest in me and deeply invested in my life—they served as a constant in a world where frequent moves were my norm. They saw the nerdy, exuberant kid and figured out how to channel all that energy and curiosity and intellectual drive. They made me gleeful and unapologetic about pursuing the life of the mind.

A study from Gallup posited that the university you attend is not as important to your success in life as the relationship you have with professors.[1] I didn't really need a survey to tell me that, but I'm glad to have the proof. My undergraduate experience at a comprehensive state university with teachers who poured their time and talent into me as a student had convinced me of that long ago. Here's just one example: though I had only one course with her (but I worked for her as a teaching assistant), one of my professors always had her door open, ready to, as she would say, "visit." Looking back, I am amazed at her spirit of welcome—she never seemed hurried or rushed or too busy. She exhibited such hospitality: At the back of her office, her coffeepot was never empty. And she kept a special tin full of cookies, just for me. With such evident joy, it's no surprise she had an office full every day with a raucous gathering of folks, the air blue with smoke (back in the days when people still smoked inside) and witty conversation. She was a proud daughter of the canyonlands of New Mexico—and I have seldom met anyone who carried herself with such easy, unapologetic confidence. From her I learned the winsomeness of authenticity, the absolute rejection of the pretentious, and the embrace, instead, of the ridiculous. When I think of our conversations through the years, the thing I remember most often is our laughter. Despite her good humor and personal warmth, she had incredible standards as a teacher—about which she was unremorseful. In that, she modeled for me a way of teaching I've made my own—that an expectation of excellence is not antithetical to a classroom full of great delight.

She is but one example of the hospitality, real and intellectual, that I received as a student. I always hope I can live up to those extraordinary people who taught me and in my own teaching carry forward their legacies, an acknowledgment of the words of Psalm 16: "The boundary lines have fallen for me in pleasant places; surely I have a delightful inheritance." Teaching, then, is an embodiment of gratitude, if you will. We love because we were first loved (1 Jn 4:19), we teach because others first taught us with care.

This book grew out of my commitments as a teacher, both in the college classroom and in public teaching venues (Sunday schools, community reading groups, the Festival of Faith & Writing, virtual learning spaces). If story is the currency of our time (and I obviously believe that it is), then we need to make sure and be very attentive to how we equip others to understand and share stories well—their own and God's. After all, in some capacity we are all teachers and all learners—and every one of us is a storyteller and a story interpreter.

Think, for instance, of Matthew's rendering of the morning of the resurrection in Matthew 28:

> After the Sabbath, at dawn on the first day of the week, Mary Magdalene and the other Mary went to look at the tomb. There was a violent earthquake, for an angel of the Lord came down from heaven and, going to the tomb, rolled back the stone and sat on it. His appearance was like lightning, and his clothes were white as snow. The guards were so afraid of him that they shook and became like dead men.
>
> The angel said to the women, "Do not be afraid, for I know that you are looking for Jesus, who was crucified. He is not here; he has risen, just as he said. Come and see the place where he lay. Then go quickly and tell his disciples: 'He has risen from the dead and is going ahead of you into Galilee. There you will see him.' Now I have told you." (Mt 28:1-7)

Let's focus on the figure of what strikes me as a rather attitudinal angel. First of all, what's with the angel sitting down and hanging out after he rolls away the stone? Clearly it's not a hard effort on his part. And even though the soldiers are scared to the point of passing out (which seems pretty logical if they'd just seen this angel come down and casually whip away a ginormously heavy rock), the angel himself seems super casual as he lingers. The resurrection is effortless. No big.

But the lingering struck me as weird: you'd think the angel's assignment might be to roll away the stone and get on with the day. But no—it's clear that communicating what happened is part of the resurrection process too. Of course, Christ's resurrection doesn't depend on an absent stone—the later appearances of Jesus through doors prove that nothing can hold him. But the stone's removal is important because it makes the resurrection clear *to us*. And just in case we don't understand that symbol, the angel says to the women the equivalent of "Hey, I knew you were coming. Let me give you a tour just to make sure you get it."

The thing is we're not very quick learners. I can't tell you how often my colleagues and I lament about how we have told our students something over and again, and yet, when the time comes for that information to be applied, somehow the students haven't heard, didn't get it, weren't paying attention. And we say to each other some version of "Seriously? I must have told them a hundred times to do X and such. Don't they ever listen?" But, of course, we're just as guilty. That's pretty much the human condition. The two Marys show up convinced that Christ is still in that tomb, and the touch of incredulity in the angel's words—"He is not here; he has risen, just as he said"—suggests that like me with my students, the angel can't quite believe the women didn't act on what they had been told, that they didn't really believe what Jesus had told them so many times. But here is a profound pedagogical principle (not surprising from Jesus, whom Mary Magdalene immediately calls Rabboni, teacher): it is that hearing is never enough—intellectual assent is transformed into belief through lived experience. Come, see, look.

The part I was most surprised by, however, and the part I think I like best is when the angel declares, "Now I have told you." What an odd thing to say. What does that mean? It sounds somewhat dismissive, somewhat impatient. A version of "Okay, my work here is done—move along." But maybe that's exactly what it does mean: the angel's job *is* done, and now it's the women's job to begin spreading the very good news to the other disciples, and for the women and the other disciples to begin living in a post-resurrection reality. With "now I have told you," the angel puts the responsibility squarely on Jesus' followers to continue the work of rolling the stone away and revealing Jesus' miraculous defeat of death.

Lingering at the tomb is not on the day's agenda. Teaching, in its broadest sense, is! After all, the *Oxford English Dictionary* lists the oldest definitions of *teach* not as imparting information or giving instruction, but as providing direction:

1. to show, present or offer a view

2. to show or point out (a thing, the way, a place) to a person

3. to direct, conduct, convoy, guide; to send away

I like these earlier definitions as metaphors of what teaching can be: helping folks to see something new, to guide them on their way, to assist them in being attentive to "the thing, the way, a place" as they journey. Even better, it's not up to us to have all the answers: the *Oxford English Dictionary* provides another antiquated definition from shipbuilding where, according to the example provided from W. H. Smyth's 1867 *Sailor's Word-book*, "To *Teach*, in marine architecture, is applied to the direction which any line or curve seems to point out." In other words, teaching is following the line to where it is naturally going to go. The job, then, is the journey— surely an attainable objective for each of us to help narrate.

FINAL EXAMS

What matters most for good teachers, then, is twofold: their attitudes toward themselves and their attitudes toward their fellow learners. I use that last phrase, *fellow learners*, rather than *students* quite deliberately because it is important for people who presume to teach to continue to cultivate the humility of learning themselves. During the pandemic, for example, teachers have been called upon to provide lessons across multiple platforms (online, in person, asynchronously). Being forced to teach in such radically different ways has made professors learners again. We're always adding to our knowledge base, but in this case, by learning new technologies, devising new ways of course delivery, reconfiguring course content, one is reminded of how difficult learning can be, how many failures it takes before one gets it right. For those of us in the senior ranks of the professoriate, it's a good reminder of how long it takes to master a *new* body of knowledge—something, perhaps, that we have not had to do for a number of years. In that way, we share more in common with students than we have in a long time. That seems like a good thing.

But even with the *old* body of knowledge that we are trying to convey, teachers need to find a way to keep it fresh for themselves. After years with the same text (and that can include our interaction with the Bible, even if we aren't literature professors), it can become easy to be glib or begin to fail to see the wonder and challenge presented. But literature matters most when it speaks into our lives. On a final exam in my global literature course, I wanted students to have some place to reflect on the ways the *Divine Comedy* had connected with them, so the final question was this: "What are three spiritual takeaways for you from reading the *Divine Comedy*?" I thought it only fair that I should answer my own question. Here are my answers.

1. Don't be afraid. Dante the Pilgrim is characterized throughout much of the poem by fear. He swoons, he hesitates, he is constantly looking to his guides (whether Virgil or Beatrice). But in canto II of *Inferno*—in other words, at almost the poem's very beginning—

he is told the story of how Virgil was sent to rescue him from the dark wood where he, the Pilgrim, has gone astray. Turns out that Beatrice has left heaven to fetch Virgil to accompany him on the first part of his journey. There is surprise that she "dared" to make the trip—how was she not afraid to travel through hell? Her reply:

I shall explain in simple words, she said,

just why I have no fear of coming here.

A man must stand in fear of just those things

that truly have the power to do us harm,

of nothing else, for nothing else is fearsome.[2]

In other words, Beatrice understands that the redeemed person can be bold because hell has no authority. Anxiety needn't control us. And in the same way that, for Dante, sin is a reordering of love, so spiritual bravery comes as a result of reordered fear, rightly understood.

2. Love in abundance. As Dante moves through purgatory, he asks many questions about how we can be made right with God. At one point, he muses about the sufficiency of God's love—how can there really be enough for all? In reply, Virgil provides a stunning image:

That infinite, ineffable true Good

that dwells in Heaven speeds instantly to love,

as light rays to a shining surface would;

just as much ardor as it finds, it gives:

the greater the proportion of our love,

the more eternal goodness we receive;

the more souls there above who are in love

the more there are worth loving; love grows more,

each soul a mirror mutually mirroring.[3]

God's love, then, is a great light—and all who love God are mirrors. As God's light shines on us, it bounces off our mirrors and amplifies God's love. And in loving each other—in bouncing God's light off our mirror into someone else's—we help to increase the light overall. What I love here, especially, is the idea that by reflecting God's light, we help in God's work of illuminating the darkness. We keep holding up our mirrors to each other to show not ourselves, but the light of God. In so doing, everything is brighter and clearer and lovelier.

3. God's got this. Interestingly, in *Paradiso* Dante wrestles with some of his most difficult theological questions. Indeed, the closer he gets to God, the more he engages with the mysteries of the faith: predestination, election, justice. (There's a clear lesson in that, I think.) In Dante's systematically arranged universe, paradise, too, has divisions (though Beatrice tries to explain that these are more metaphorical than anything). These levels of heaven bother Dante the Pilgrim profoundly—so much so that he asks Piccarda, a nun who broke her vows, if she isn't a little resentful at not being in a different part of paradise:

But tell me: all you souls so happy here,

do you yearn for a higher post in Heaven,

to see more, to become more loved by Him?

She gently smiled, as did the other shades;

then came her words so full of happiness,

she seemed to glow with the first fire of love:

Brother, the virtue of our heavenly love,

tempers our will and makes us want no more

than what we have—we thirst for this alone.

If we desired to be higher up,

then our desires would not be in accord

with His will Who assigns us to this sphere;

. . . . in His will is our peace.[4]

"In His will is our peace." What a profound statement of contentment. Piccarda knows that God's love doesn't depend on our location. There is no place where God isn't. But even more than that, she rests in the knowledge that she has been put in the exact perfect place for her in God's well-ordered world. No wonder Piccarda smiles.

It feels right to take a "final exam" every once in a while to remind ourselves what we're learning too. In fact, to ensure that we *are* learning. And to make that visible to our students as an act of teacherly modesty. Like the Bereans, who the book of Acts commends to us because they studied the Scriptures together to make sure they were reliable, we seek to learn together, from one another.

Such a model is also why I am grateful to teach in a department and at a university with a strong commitment to all of us teaching "gen ed" students with the same commitment and quality with which we teach our majors. Even as a tenured full professor, I still relish teaching intro classes—first-year composition and core literature. At many institutions, faculty at my rank and level of experience (read: old) would rarely, if ever, have these courses on their schedules. Indeed, many in academe have traditionally seen the movement away from intro classes as a reward. And to be sure, they are hard classes to teach—much harder in many ways than classes in one's specialty. Which is exactly why I believe the most experienced professors should be teaching a sizable percentage of them.

Why? First, they remind me of the joy of learning. I adore the enthusiasm of first-year students. Even when they are scared and overwhelmed by all that is new in the college experience, they are raring to get going to change the world. They've got a million ideas and the idealism to match. In a world where cynicism can be a default, they are a tonic. They're also so talented (even as they don't always see it in themselves fully yet—which is also charming) that I can never despair about the future.

Second, I get to extend hospitality like that extended to me. I get the honor of being one of the people who helps students learn how to "do" college. Intro classes—especially something like first-year writing—are not simply about academic content but about teaching habits of mind and instilling modes of self-discipline that will bring students success beyond the gen ed classroom. It's giving students ways of being, instilling a lifelong curiosity and love of knowledge and, hopefully, a little confidence in themselves as learners, too. And maybe convincing them that they could like subjects (writing and literature) for which they may think they have little aptitude. Certainly, first-year students can be naive and clueless (and prone to not read the syllabus)—but no one comes to college knowing how it all works. Education is not ever just the what, but the why and the how and the when. And everyone needs a guide to encourage and inspire.

Third, I'm reminded of the fundamentals. I love introducing students to the broad sweep of literature and to the power of story, to the magnitude of language and to themselves as meaning makers. Here is where we get to invite students into the wonder of our disciplines. Here is where we get to equip them to begin to think and write well. Here is where we get to challenge them to grapple with difficult concepts and difficult texts. And here *we* get challenged professionally to see if we can communicate the essentials to smart young people. Anyone can lament about "kids these days" and all they don't know—but to connect core subjects with what students actually bring to the college classroom and make those subjects relevant and meaningful is a much more difficult task. Few things are as rewarding, though.

Fourth, I get to keep learning. Like many teachers, I started off teaching people not that much younger than I was. Those days were now very long ago. Instead, every year brings students who come with contexts of which I have little to no experience. (That was probably always true, but our pop-culture connections perhaps obscured deeper diversities.) The joy of having students who come out of so many different backgrounds—and often who have nothing in common with me in terms of intellectual or any other kind of interests—is that each class brings new eyes and hearts to our work. Indeed, I have never had a semester pass when students did not help me see anew the subjects to which I have devoted my life.

One of my favorite hymns has always been "O God Our Help in Ages Past." For a long time, the song mostly made me reflect on the possession of a "goodly" heritage—in the long history of Christendom or in the testimony of those who have gone before. But the older I get, the more I think about the next line. In teaching at a faith-based institution, I share in the "ages past" with my students, but it is in our time together in the classroom as they prepare to do God's work in God's world that the assurance of "our hope for years to come" shines brightest. My attitude as a teacher means I see us all working together in that unbroken line, bending toward God's final redemption.

LET IT SNOW

Or think about the words of Psalm 145:4, "One generation commends your works to another; they tell of your mighty acts." I used to hear this as a one-way verse describing the older generations' job to testify to the younger. Looking at it again, I think that's much too limited. Certainly, older folks have a role to tell of faithfulness along the long road, but what if we listened to what younger generations were commending to us about the "mighty acts" they see God doing? What might be revealed? How might our vision of church change? In other words, how does listening as teachers help us cultivate godly attitudes toward our fellow learners?

Because, let's be honest, criticism is more often the norm. It's very fashionable these days to bemoan the awfulness of the current crop of self-absorbed (insert your generational group here, be they millennial, post-millennial, Gen Y, Gen Z, whatever). I see younger folks get mocked for their "fragility." But it *is* a fragile time—if one is a beginning student, it's not wrong to acknowledge that the early years of college can be trying ones—so much change, so many new stresses, so much struggle with big ideas and big demands. Students mess up, miss deadlines, procrastinate, self-sabotage. After all my years in the classroom, I've seen most things before, but of course, for students this is their first time through—and it can feel calamitous. And even beyond the first year of college, students need truth and grace in careful balance from us folks who are walking alongside. Students need to be given space to try and fail. And fail again. And if we who teach are given the opportunity to speak into an emerging adult's life in an office hour or a mentoring session, we should count it only privilege, not get annoyed because they don't know better already.

Recently, I met a large group of incoming students at my university's first-year-students orientation session. They were all bright, eager, respectful—and excited to be starting their college experience. They seemed kind, engaged, smart. Many stayed behind after my presentation to say hello, shake my hand, thank me for my words. In short, they were lovely. Maybe it's odd to say that college students are lovely. Nobody seems to much. Indeed, when I googled "what's wrong with college students today," I got forty-eight million hits. We're told that they are entitled, they are overly fixated on their phones and social media, they need instant gratification, they all want a trophy because they participated. They are narcissistic selfie-takers and precious snowflakes, unprepared and undereducated for the rigors of life and school. Clearly, we *can't even* with this bunch. Bring back the good old days when people actually did the assigned reading, right?

The problem is I'm not sure when that golden age was. You'll know from earlier chapters that my favorite novel is George Eliot's *Middlemarch*. I traveled to England for an international conference commemorating Eliot's bicentennial, where I presented a paper on teaching that novel. In my preparatory research, I came across an essay by a very distinguished scholar who characterized *her* students thus:

> Modern American students reading *Middlemarch* usually have no equivalent frame of reference to bring to their study. Surrounded by electronic gadgetry of every description— television sets, VCRs, Walkmans, and boomboxes—they more often than not have little or no knowledge of the classics, mythology, foreign language, history, or the nineteenth century and its social or political issues. They often bring in-different reading skills to their tasks. This observation should not be construed as a criticism of students: they are neces-sarily the products of their times and the laxness of the current American educational system.[5]

Some of the technology references probably give it away, but the essay was not written recently. In fact, it was written in 1990: the year *I* graduated from college. This, then, is a description of my late-1980s generation: distracted by technology, bad readers, "products of their times and the laxness of the current American educational system." Clearly, such has it ever been.

And yet, post-millennials *are* different in some important regards from those of us who came before: for one thing, they are more diverse and better-educated. A Pew Research Center's study found that not only are 48 percent of American post-millennials racial or ethnic minorities, but as a group, they are pursuing college at higher rates than previous generations.[6] The always fascinating "Mindset List," now administered by Marist College, is an excellent reminder of what these college students' childhoods were actually like: they've always had Wi-Fi and Google, they've never licked a stamp, their every moment was videotaped by camcorder-clutching parents. Why would posting to Instagram be weird when your parents had already "curated" every day of your life so far?

Perhaps the criticism post-millennials receive, however, is that they are "snowflakes"—too sensitive for their own good. It's true that this generational cohort seems less resilient and reports record rates of anxiety, depression, and loneliness. Another Pew study found that three in ten teens feel tense, nervous or wish they had more friends every single day.[7] Publications such as *The Chronicle of Higher Education* regularly report on the "anxiety crisis" in American universities, finding in August 2022 that "at the beginning of 2021, three-fourths of students in bachelor's programs and two-thirds of adults seeking associate's degrees had considered taking a break from college due to emotional stress."[8] And, the Healthy Mind Study in Fall 2020 noted, for example, that 39 percent of students reported depression, 34 percent reported an anxiety disorder, and 53 percent reported "mental health therapy/counseling and/or psychiatric medication" within the previous year.[9] We need to not dismiss or diminish the mental health issues that need to be addressed.

Instead of evoking criticism, this kind of suffering saddens and sobers me. I'm grateful that our campus takes so seriously our call to come alongside students whether in the classroom or dorm, chapel or counseling center. But I'm puzzled by more typical media responses of ridicule and dismissal, of eye-rolling and "kids these days." It's time to think about how and why this beautiful, brilliant generation is so full of fear. Maybe it's because during my time in high school, we had one bomb threat that everyone took as a prank (it was), but during Gen Z's lifetime so far it has been Columbine and Sandy Hook and Marjory Stoneman Douglas and Uvalde (and that's a tiny fraction and only the schools, not the churches and synagogues, theaters and Walmart stores, concerts and festivals). I practiced hiding occasionally under my desk for tornadoes, never for an active shooter. Hijackings happened infrequently, but no one slammed planes into buildings when I was a kindergartener. We were told to "give a hoot, don't pollute," not face an imminent future where climate change would bring massive ecological devastation. We went to college generously underwritten by the taxpayers and left with little or no debt, instead of coping with the biggest state defunding of higher education in decades. Diplomacy seems to be dead, religion is fast losing any credible witness, institutions are failing, the economy wobbles, hate predominates—anxiety seems like a pretty rational response, to be honest.

What I love about my college students, what makes me so hopeful and so happy to work with them, is that anxiety isn't their only response: I'm impressed that they still care deeply about the world, even when they're seeing it in a very sorry state. I'm impressed that they are excited to prepare themselves to make that world better. I'm impressed how they care deeply about and for each other as well as for the marginalized and the oppressed. And I'm impressed that they care deeply about suffering and injustice—

and want to make it right. They crave authenticity and connection and a faith that animates life, not one that's about acquisitions or power or social status or membership in a sociological club.

They're calling us to attention. What a privilege! Like every class of students I've had, they remain delightfully energetic, eager to make a difference. As a generation, they are tenderhearted toward each other and toward the world. Like every generation, when we invite them into the extraordinary project of loving God with our minds, they are curious and creative and full of compassion for God's world. And ready to get to work.

Because if these generations' insistence on kindness and concern and compassion makes them snowflakes, I say, let it snow!

BAREFOOT TEACHING

As we consider how to urge each other on to the very best engagement with story—as tellers, listeners, and interpreters—I want to conclude with some essential principles for how we approach each other as we do this work. What if instead of bemoaning what learners aren't, we emphasize what they are?

At the conclusion of each of his courses, my late friend Dale Brown always ended with a poem. Often it was one of his favorites, Richard Wilbur's "The Writer." As the poem begins, a father hears his young daughter typing a story in her bedroom and stops to listen. Rather than dismiss her because of her age, he instead empathetically appreciates the importance of what she is writing and feeling. As he continues to listen, he thinks back to a scene two years before when a starling had become trapped in his daughter's bedroom, and he and his daughter worked and worked to try and help the bird escape. The bird made a myriad of agonizingly unsuccessful tries, but the delight was keen when the bird finally got free. More than that, the bird's escape reminds the father of how fraught

the world is, how much his writing daughter faces—and he again
blesses her, but this time with a greater fervor:

It is always a matter, my darling,

Of life or death, as I had forgotten. I wish

What I wished you before, but harder.[10]

For me, the poem beautifully encapsulates so much of what I
admire about Dale's aims in the classroom. Like the father, Dale
listened carefully to his students and what they were trying to ex-
press. He took them seriously, never laughing at them or dismissing
their ideas or their concerns because of their age—he understood
that they felt things intensely. Even when they were discovering
insights that were new only to them, he was patient and gentle in
guiding them. He knew that, like the bird, students might need
multiple tries to fly successfully—and that the effort might be a
painful one for them. Yet he also believed in the innate beauty of
each student—and the joy in watching each take flight. What he
was teaching them was powerful stuff—"life or death," indeed—no
easy answers. But there was never any mistake that Dale's fervent
good wishes for them were foremost in the discussion. That is vital.

For me, moreover, wherever or whatever I teach, teaching well
means connecting with students and convincing them that they
and their learning matter to me as the teacher. It's about cultivating
a conversation built on mutuality. In fact, teaching is so deeply
relational that when a class seems like mere content delivery, something very profound is lost. That one can connect with students in
a large number of ways is certainly true—whether I'm interacting
with students on a discussion board, through an email, over a video
connection, or during an in-class discussion. However it happens,
though, it is the students' humanity, the recognition that one is
interacting with beloved children, images of God, that needs to lie

at the heart of our connection. These are my brothers and sisters as much as they are my students.

In the classroom, then, I want to practice incarnational pedagogy, making sure that what I say matches what I do (knowing that the task will demand humility and grace as I fail to live up to my own ideals more often than I would like). That I enflesh my words with the kind of teaching I would hope bears witness to my deepest beliefs. Yes, there's a good deal of content I aim to cover with them, too. But whatever content they take away (or don't), here's what I hope my students hear most.

You are loved. Nothing you will do or be will make you more beloved by God. You are so welcome here, and I am genuinely excited to see what God will do in and through you. *Noli timere*: don't be afraid.

You are enough. George Eliot says it this way: "The blessed work of helping the world forward, happily does not wait to be done by perfect men."[11] Or as my late mother often directed: "Look around and see what needs to be done." Usually, Platonic ideals do not accomplish much, nor do expectations that we or others need to be just so. Your performance here does not define your essence. Good or bad, it is not who you are nor does it measure your worth as a human being or the affection and respect with which I hold you. And nothing can separate you from the love of God.

I want you to succeed. Too often, students come into an English class already decided that they are bad at writing or at literary interpretation. Grammar or organization or analysis has eluded them in the past—and their confidence may be low. And though they certainly might not be as proficient as they could be, I want them to understand that I am not here to reinforce what they can't do but to show them how they can thrive. All professors know that it's super easy to write an assignment or exam that shows what students don't know—I want students to know that I expect them to succeed because I know they can. And I tell them so.

Your voice matters. And why do I want them to succeed? Because we need every single one of their voices in our civic life, in our churches, in the places where we work, in our broader communities. They may feel like their voice is too small, too inconsequential. And yes, the writing we'll be doing in class is hard because thinking is hard, nuance is hard, conversation and engagement are hard. But like any workout, the longer one exercises, the fitter one becomes. I want students who ultimately are fearless in speaking truth, in speaking consolation and restoration, in speaking hope. In bringing more words of life the world is desperate for.

What if these were the criteria by which we engaged everyone—not just students—who is navigating their story?

So much could be said about all that makes teaching such a high calling and great responsibility (as the apostle James reminds us in James 3:1), such a necessity in a world where people need reliable guides to come alongside them and help in understanding their own narratives. But perhaps an image to leave with: when I visited the exquisite fifth-century mosaics in the Italian city of Ravenna, I saw a scene that encapsulates how we might approach teaching. Up on the wall, the story of Moses and the burning bush became "Moses and the burning bushes." Not one bush: no, the mosaic showed the whole hillside, in the words of chapter two's epigraph, with "every common bush afire with God" and Moses as the one "who sees, takes off his shoes."

We do not meet to do ordinary work when we come to the classroom (or work together to learn through story more generally). Instead, like every other square inch, it is holy, heaven-crammed ground. If we are teachers or professors, we get the amazing opportunity of helping students "see" and by our own posture, modeling humble attentiveness. Teaching is such a challenging job because, while it is concentrated on the immediate (that is, focused on the information and skills we need to learn today), it is, at its best, also always forward looking. What do students need for their lives as they leave the classroom? What habits of heart and mind will be portable? How can we make sure the time in the classroom really matters?

These questions can be vexing ones. My late colleague Lionel Basney once wrote a poem in which a professor questions whether giving his life to teaching has really been worth it. In the professor's vision, he meets a guide who reassures him by saying:

You cannot know . . . what your words

will weigh with students remembering them

in a place you will never see.[12]

And that's the point, isn't it? "You cannot know" because we work in the present, we work "as unto the Lord," but never seeing the full flowering of our efforts.

But the wonderful implication is that students *will* remember—just in ways and in places we will never know about. And that's actually the most exciting part of all: we can't even imagine where our students will go and what they will do. Thanks be to God that God only asks us to serve faithfully—and amazes us "throughout all generations" with the results. The promise of Ephesians 3:20-21 reminds us that God always has bigger plans for our gifts than we can ever fathom. When we do use them well, we bear witness to God in his creation and in our students, everyone, "afire" with God's image. Our hope as teachers is to send forth a shoeless generation, full of wonder, to continue to share the greatest story ever told.

Acknowledgments

ONE OF THE LESSONS OF AGE is how very little gets done without a huge network of support. That's certainly true for me in the writing of this book. I've always loved Emily Dickinson's formulation "my friends are my estate" because it captures how very rich I feel every day. My gratitude to everyone in my community—colleagues, students, friends—who helped make this book possible. Many, many people at work (thanks to all my students who sharpened my thinking and to stalwart colleagues), at church (special shout-out to Lindsey Lugo, who always asked me about the book whenever she saw me), and online (yes, I appreciated every single kind comment on Facebook, Twitter, and Instagram)—all of you were so graciously encouraging.

And I'm so grateful to you, dear reader, for spending your time with this book. I am humbled that you would give me the honor of your attention. I hope at least some small thing in the book has given you better ways to think about yourself and the importance of your story.

My thinking for this book has developed over the years in my role as a regular blogger on *The 12/Reformed Journal*. My thanks to Steve Mathonnet-VanderWell and Jeff Munroe both for overseeing the blog and for allowing me to step away for many months to write this book. My talented student, Olivia Mason, was my expert substitute in my months away—my thanks to her for that gift.

To be honest, I hadn't been planning on writing a book at all, but the wonderful Natalie Rowland kept bugging me about it, and eventually her incredible belief that I might have something to say propelled me to get my act together. A visit with one of my heroes, Katherine Paterson, when she told me it was time for me to "write my own stories," gave me the extra encouragement that I needed. Throughout the project, Natalie and Katherine both kept up their cheerleading—for which I am enormously indebted.

My editor, David McNutt, was invaluable in helping to envision what this book might look like. His kind guidance throughout has been deeply appreciated. The staff at IVP—from the talented designer of the book's cover through the savvy marketing team to the diligent copyeditor—were a delight to work with. Subaas Gurung patiently helped me navigate the many permissions this book required. I acknowledge here my profound appreciation for a grant from the Calvin Center for Christian Scholarship to defray the cost of the permissions. Thanks to Dean for Research David Wunder and Margie Styf for expertly facilitating that process. And I'm absolutely delighted that my favorite singer-songwriter, Carrie Newcomer, gave permission for the use of one of her beautifully thoughtful compositions—thank you, Carrie!

I've also benefited from some very practical assistance: my wonderful colleague, Karin Maag, brought her status as a leading scholar of John Calvin to help me identify an errant Calvin quote. And the extraordinary Abigail Ham provided much-needed proofreading of the manuscript (any errors are, of course, on me). More than that (and that was a lot), however, her exceptionally capable work as my assistant for the academic journal I edit and for the department I chair made my life while writing the book possible. I could not have done it without her.

The book begins and ends talking about teachers, and as the book notes, I have been very blessed in the many teachers who invested in my life. Three of my college professors, in particular, set me on the path toward being a professor myself with their selfless mentoring, and I want to honor the memory here of Lynn Moncus and Darlis Miller. Harriet Kramer Linkin has been my wise and enthusiastic guide since the very first class I took with her in 1987. Over thirty-five years on, I cherish all she has continued to be in my life.

I am quite fierce in my conviction that I am compassed round by the very best of friends. There are too many to name (please, friends, consider yourselves all thanked!), but a special gratitude to those who read parts of the book in manuscript and/or propped me up throughout the process: Roy and Ellen Anker, Cheryl Brandsen, Gayle Brown, Gayle Ermer, Mary Hulst, Kristine Johnson, Beth and Mark Koster, Andrea Le Roy, Leslie Mathews, Debra Rienstra, Marcy Taylor, Sarah Turnage, Debbie Visser. For her assistance in writing and in life, my compatriot and dear buddy, Jane Zwart, deserves to have it said of her, as Dante said of Arnault Daniel and Eliot said of Pound, that she is *il miglior fabbro*.

Finally, I remember here with love and thanksgiving my late mother, Sally, and my late grandparents, Aimee Kline and Grace and Elmer Holberg. What a goodly heritage! Enormous thanks to my brother, John Holberg, and my sister, Jane Wierenga (and my lovely brother-in-law Mark and beloved nieces, Grace and Sally), not just for support but their permission to share some of our family's stories here. Y'all are the best!

This book is dedicated to my father, Ben Holberg. Words are insufficient to convey my thanks for his righteous example, his never-ending encouragement, his persistent witness to the goodness of God. He has taught me to say: to God be the glory!

Notes

1. COMPLICATED NARRATIVES AND IMPORTANT FAILURES

[1] Andrew Malcolm, "Elizabeth Edwards Speaks, Gently, on Her Cancer, Husband's Affair," *Los Angeles Times*, September 22, 2008, https://latimesblogs.latimes.com /washington/2008/09/elizabeth-edwar.html.

[2] Percy Bysshe Shelley, "Defense of Poetry," in *Essays, Letters from Abroad, Translations and Fragments* (London: Edward Moxon, 1840).

[3] Henry Zylstra, *Testament of Vision* (Grand Rapids, MI: Eerdmans, 1958), 87.

[4] J. Todd Billings and Christian Wiman, "A Poet & a Theologian Talk About Incurable Cancer," September 14, 2015, Western Theological Seminary, Holland, MI, video recording, https://vimeo.com/123866178?embedded=true&source= video_title&owner=14177254.

[5] Frederick Buechner, *Beyond Words* (San Francisco: HarperSanFrancisco, 2004), 379.

[6] Marilynne Robinson, "Psalm Eight," in *The Death of Adam: Essays on Modern Thought* (New York: Picador, 1998), 243.

[7] Flannery O'Connor, "The Church and the Fiction Writer," *Collected Works* (New York: Library of America, 1988), 809.

[8] O'Connor, "Church and the Fiction Writer," 811.

[9] O'Connor, "Church and the Fiction Writer," 811-12.

[10] Katherine Paterson, The Buechner Institute Annual Lectureship, King College (now University), January 29, 2011, Bristol, TN.

[11] Dante, *Inferno*, trans. Mark Musa (New York: Penguin, 1995), 1.1.

[12] Dante, *The Divine Comedy: Inferno*, trans. John Ciardi (New York: Modern Library, 1996), 12.40.

[13] Dante, *The Divine Comedy: Inferno*, trans. Henry Wadsworth Longfellow (New York: Modern Library, 2004).

[14] T. S. Eliot, "Burnt Norton," in *Four Quartets* (New York: Harvest Harcourt, 1971), 101.

[15]John Calvin, *Institutes of the Christian Religion* Vol. I, ed. John T. McNeill, trans. Ford Lewis Battles (Louisville: Westminster John Knox, 1960), 52, 61.

[16]Calvin, *Institutes*, 61.

[17]W. H. Auden, "Musée des Beaux Arts," in *Collected Poems* (New York: Random House, 1968).

2. ENOUGH

[1]For a fuller accounting of Brueggemann's thinking, see Walter Brueggemann, *The Prophetic Imagination*, 2nd ed. (Minneapolis, MN: Fortress Press), 2001.

[2]Frederick Buechner, *The Sacred Journey* (San Francisco: HarperSanFrancisco, 1982), 46.

[3]This idea is suffused throughout Makoto Fujimura's book *Art and Faith: A Theology of Making* (New Haven: Yale University Press, 2020).

[4]Mary Oliver, "Mindful," *Devotions: The Selected Poems of Mary Oliver* (New York: Penguin, 2017), 173-74.

[5]John Calvin, *Sermons sur les chapitres X et XI de la première epitre aux Corinthiens* in *Joannis Calvini Opera Quae Supersunt Omnia*, Wilhelm Baum, Eduard Cunitz, Eduard Reuss, eds. (Braunschweig: Schwetschke & Sons, 1892) 49: col. 698.

[6]Mary Oliver, "Mindful," 173-74.

[7]Gerard Manley Hopkins, "Pied Beauty," in *Poems of Gerard Manley Hopkins*, ed. Robert Bridges (London: Humphrey Milford, 1918).

[8]Matthew Arnold, "The Buried Life," in *Poetry and Criticism of Matthew Arnold*, ed. A. Dwight Culler (Boston: Houghton Mifflin, 1961), 113-15.

[9]Email correspondence with the author, April 18, 2004.

[10]Shari Tishman, *Slow Looking: The Art and Practice of Learning Through Observation* (New York: Routledge, 2018), 2.

[11]Alexandra Horowitz, *On Looking: A Walker's Guide to the Art of Observation* (New York: Scribner, 2013).

[12]Kate Bowler, *Blessed: A History of the American Prosperity Gospel* (Oxford: Oxford University Press, 2013); Kate Bowler, *Everything Happens for a Reason: And Other Lies I've Loved* (New York: Random House, 2018).

[13]Gerard Manley Hopkins, "That Nature Is a Heraclitean Fire and of the Comfort of the Resurrection," in *Poems of Gerard Manley Hopkins*, ed. Robert Bridges (London: Humphrey Milford, 1918).

[14]Daniel W. Graham, "Heraclitus," in *The Stanford Encyclopedia of Philosophy* (Summer 2021 Edition), ed. Edward N. Zalta, https://plato.stanford.edu/archives/sum2021/entries/heraclitus/.

3. GRACED WITH THE ORDINARY

[1]George Eliot, *Middlemarch* (Oxford: Oxford University Press, 1998).

[2]Virginia Woolf, "George Eliot," *Times Literary Supplement*, November 20, 1919.

[3]Eliot, *Middlemarch*, 3.

[4]Eliot, *Middlemarch*, 785.

[5]Mary Oliver, "The Summer's Day," in *Devotions* (New York: Penguin, 2017), 316.

[6]Mary Oliver, "Summer Morning," in *Red Bird* (Boston: Beacon Press, 2008), 30.

[7]*They Shall Not Grow Old*, produced and directed by Peter Jackson (Burbank, CA: Warner Bros., 2018).

[8]Mary Oliver, "In the Storm," in *Thirst* (Boston: Beacon Press, 2006), 62.

[9]*Oxford English Dictionary* online, third ed., s.v., "miracle," accessed December 10, 2022, www.oed.com.

[10]One example of Hannibal Buress performing this bit: Hannibal Buress, "Your Prayers Mean Nothing," Just for Laughs Festival 2011, YouTube video uploaded June 29, 2016, www.youtube.com/watch?v=hHUNPS0BzYc.

[11]Barbara Brown Taylor, *Speaking of Sin* (Cambridge, MA: Cowley, 2000), 96.

[12]Jane Zwart, "On Beauty and Being Just," in *32 Poems*, vol. 18.1 (Spring/Summer 2020).

[13]George Eliot, *Middlemarch* (Oxford: Oxford University Press, 1998), 398.

[14]Eliot, *Middlemarch*, 399.

[15]Mark Magnier, "Suu Kyi's Piano Tuners Play Small but Key Part in Myanmar History," *Los Angeles Times*, November 15, 2012.

[16]Frank Bruni, "George Bush and the Obituary Wars," *New York Times*, December 4, 2018, www.nytimes.com/2018/12/04/opinion/george-hw-bush-obituary.html.

[17]Bruni, "George Bush."

[18]William Wordsworth, "Lines Written a Few Miles Above Tintern Abbey," in *William Wordsworth: The Major Works* (Oxford: Oxford University Press, 1984), 131-35.

[19]Elizabeth Gaskell, *Cranford* (Oxford: Oxford University Press, 2011), 158.

[20]A. P. Carter, "This World Is Not My Home, I'm Just a Passing Through," 1937, https://hymnary.org/text/this_world_is_not_my_home_im_just_a

[21]George Herbert, "The Windows," in *The English Poems of George Herbert*, ed. C. A. Patrides (London: Everyman, 1974), 84-85.

[22]Robert MacFarlane (@RobGMacFarlane), 2018, "Word of the day: 'witness-tree' - originally a tree that stood as a record of property boundaries, marked as such by scores in its bark. Now broadened to mean a tree that has seen remarkable things, that stands as 'a repository for the past.'" Twitter, January 21, 2018, https://twitter.com/robgmacfarlane/status/954979420883881984.

[23]Sarah Lindsay, "If God Made Jam," in *Debt to the Bone-Eating Snotflower* (Port Townsend, WA: Copper Canyon, 2013).

[24]Marilynne Robinson, "Psalm Eight," in *The Death of Adam: Essays on Modern Thought* (New York, Picador, 1998), 243.

4. ASSESSING THE HILL

[1]Kathleen Norris, *The Quotidian Mysteries: Laundry, Liturgy, and "Women's Work"* (New York: Paulist, 1998).

[2]Morgan Greene, "Betsy Ebeling, friend to many including Hillary Clinton, dies at 72," *Chicago Tribune*, July 30, 2019, www.chicagotribune.com/news/breaking/ct-betsy-ebeling-obituary-20190730-rd6fo5y5mzfvfasgsaawaclbrm-story.html.

[3]Susan Mettes, *The Loneliness Epidemic: Why So Many of Us Feel Alone—and How Leaders Can Respond* (Grand Rapids, MI: Brazos, 2021).

[4]Billy Baker, "The Biggest Threat Facing Middle-Age Men Isn't Smoking or Obesity. It's Loneliness," *Boston Globe*, March 9, 2017.

[5]Frederick Buechner, *Whistling in the Dark* (San Francisco: HarperCollins, 1993), 54-55.

[6]Natalie Angier, "African Tribesmen Can Talk Birds into Helping Them Find Honey," *New York Times*, July 22, 2016, www.nytimes.com/2016/07/23/science/birds-bees-honeyguides-africa.html?smid=tw-share.

[7]Harper Lee, "Christmas to Me," in *McCalls*, 1961, https://web.archive.org/web/20070701015651/www.chebucto.ns.ca/culture/HarperLee/christmas.html.

[8]Russell Shorto, "The Woman Who Made van Gogh," *New York Times Magazine*, April 14, 2021.

[9]Simone Schnall, Kent D. Harber, Jeanine K. Stefanucci, and Dennis R. Proffitt, "Social Support and the Perception of Geographical Slant," *J Exp Soc Psychol* 44, no. 5 (September 2008): 1246-55, www.ncbi.nlm.nih.gov/pmc/articles/PMC3291107.

[10]Carol Zaleski, "An Open Heart," in *Christian Century*, vol. 120, no. 24 (November 2003), 33.

[11]Emily Dickinson, "Letter for Samuel Bowles: 1858," in *The Select Poems and Letters of Emily Dickinson*, ed. Robert N. Linscott (Garden City, NY: Doubleday Anchor Books, 1959), 270.

5. A WITNESS READY TO SERVE

[1]Calvin University, "Educational Framework," accessed December 15, 2020, https://calvin.edu/dotAsset/b9bb3ebc-077e-419a-bdcc-9993b3c4cc23.

[2]*Mrs. America*, created by Dahvi Waller, aired 2020, on Hulu.

[3]Marlo Thomas & Friends, *Free to Be . . . You and Me*, Bell Records, 1972, 33⅓ rpm.

[4]Jane Kenyon, "Finding a Long Gray Hair," in *Collected Poems* (Minneapolis: Graywolf, 2005), 14.

[5]Annie Dillard, "Living Like Weasels," in *Teaching a Stone to Talk* (New York: Harper, 1982), 65-70.

[6]T. S. Eliot, "Dry Salvages," in *Four Quartets* (New York: Harvest Harcourt, 1971), 45.

[7]*Oxford English Dictionary* online, third ed., s.v., "colleague," accessed December 10, 2022, www.oed.com.

[8]Gerald Rau, *Mapping the Origins Debate: Six Models of the Beginning of Everything* (Downers Grove, IL: InterVarsity Press, 2012).

[9]David Wagoner, "Lost," in *Poetry* (July 1971), 219.

[10]Morgan Neville, dir., *20 Feet from Stardom* (New York: RADiUS-TWC Films, 2013).

[11]The conversation is discussed in Laura McKenna, "How Hard Do Professors Actually Work?," *The Atlantic*, February 7, 2018, www.theatlantic.com/education/archive/2018/02/how-hard-do-professors-actually-work/552698/. The original article: Colleen Flaherty, "So Much to Do, So Little Time," *Inside Higher Education*, April 9, 2014, www.insidehighered.com/news/2014/04/09/research-shows-professors-work-long-hours-and-spend-much-day-meetings.

[12]Nicholas A. Christakis (@NAChristakis), 2018, "I tell my graduate students and post-docs that if they're working 60 hours per week, they're working less than the full professors, and less than their peers." Twitter, February 4, 2018, https://twitter.com/NAChristakis/status/960211767434665984.

[13]Augustine, *On Christian Teaching*, trans. R. P. H. Green (Oxford: Oxford University Press, 1997), 5-6.

6. OUR LITTLE SYSTEMS

[1]Flannery O'Connor, "The Catholic Novelist in the Protestant South," in *Collected Works* (New York: Library of America, 1988), 862.

[2]Denise Levertov, "The Tide," in *The Stream and the Sapphire* (New York: New Directions, 1997), 25-26.

[3]Denise Levertov, "Goodbye to Tolerance," in *The Collected Poems of Denise Levertov* (New York: New Directions, 2013), 468-69.

[4]N. T. Wright, "Christianity Offers No Answers About the Coronavirus. It's Not Supposed To," *Time*, March 29, 2020, https://time.com/5808495/coronavirus-christianity.

[5]Julian of Norwich, *Revelations of Divine Love*, trans. Elizabeth Spearing (New York: Penguin, 1998), 79.

[6]T. S. Eliot, "East Coker," in *Four Quartets* (New York: Harvest Harcourt, 1971), 30-31.

[7]Nicolas Wolterstorff, *Lament for a Son* (Grand Rapids: Eerdmans, 1987), 80.

[8]Eliot, "East Coker."

[9]Matthew Arnold, *Letters of Matthew Arnold*, ed. George W. E. Russell (New York: Macmillan, 1896), I:34.

[10]Charlotte Brontë, preface, *Jane Eyre*, second ed. (London: Smith, Elder, 1847).

[11]Brontë, preface, *Jane Eyre*.

[12]Christina Rossetti, "Who Shall Deliver Me," in *Poems* (Boston: Little, Brown, 1906), 283.

[13]Christina Rossetti, "Good Friday," in *Poems* (Boston: Little, Brown, 1906), 299.

[14]Stevie Smith, "Not Waving but Drowning," in *Collected Poems* (New York: New Directions, 1983), 18.

[15]Jane Kenyon, "Otherwise," in *Collected Poems* (Minneapolis: Greywolf, 2005), 266.

[16]Donald Hall, "Distressed Haiku," in *The Painted Bed* (New York: Houghton Mifflin, 2002).

[17]Alfred, Lord Tennyson, "Prologue," in *In Memoriam*, Norton Critical Edition (New York: Norton, 2020).

[18]*The Lord of the Rings: Return of the King*, directed by Peter Jackson (Burbank: CA, New Line Cinema, 2003).

7. SMALL STEPS AT VERY GREAT COST

[1]Tracy K. Smith, "An Old Story," *Wade in the Water* (Minneapolis, MN: Graywolf, 2018).

[2]W. B. Yeats, "The Second Coming," in *Michael Robartes and the Dancer* (Dublin: Cuala, 1921).

[3]Matthew Arnold, preface to *Culture and Anarchy* (London: Smith, Elder, 1869).

[4]Benjamin Fearnow, "Mick Mulvaney Says He's Surprised Supporters Took Trump 'Literally,' Riot 'Changed Everything,'" *Newsweek*, January 10, 2021, www.newsweek .com/mick-mulvaney-says-hes-surprised-supporters-took-trump-literally-riot -changed-everything-1560306.

[5]Wendell Berry, "Sabbaths 2001," in *Poetry* magazine, October 2002, 7.

[6]Katherine Paterson, "In Search of Wonder," in *The Invisible Child: On Reading and Writing Books for Children* (New York: Dutton Children's Books, 2001), 21.

[7]Frederick William Paterson, "There's a Wideness in God's Mercy," 1862, https:// hymnary.org/text/theres_a_wideness_in_gods_mercy.

[8]Elizabeth Bishop, "Questions of Travel," in *The Complete Poems, 1927-1979* (New York: Farrar, Straus and Giroux, 1983), 93.

[9]Julian of Norwich, *Revelations of Divine Love*, trans. Elizabeth Spearing (New York: Penguin, 1998), 79.

8. ROOT-ROOM

[1]Frederick Buechner, "Mark," in *Beyond Words* (San Francisco: HarperSanFrancisco, 2004), 242.

[2]John Calvin, *Commentary on the Book of Psalms*, trans. Rev. James Anderson, Christian Classics Ethereal Library (Grand Rapids, MI), https://ccel.org/ccel/calvin/calcom11/calcom11.i.html.

[3]C. S. Lewis, "Learning in War-Time," in *The Weight of Glory, and Other Addresses* (Grand Rapids, MI: Eerdmans, 1965), 43-54.

[4]Matthew Arnold, "Dover Beach," in *Poetry and Criticism of Matthew Arnold*, ed. A. Dwight Culler (Boston: Houghton Mifflin, 1961), 161.

[5]Gerard Manley Hopkins, "My Own Heart Let Me More Have Pity On," in *Poems of Gerard Manley Hopkins*, ed. Robert Bridges (London: Humphrey Milford, 1918).

[6]Charles Seymour, *Michelangelo's David: A Search for Identity* (Pittsburgh: Pittsburgh University Press, 1967), 134-37.

[7]Dante, *Purgatorio* 3.121-23, trans. Mark Musa (New York: Penguin, 1995) 133-35.

[8]Eugene Peterson, *A Long Obedience in the Same Direction* (Downers Grove, IL: InterVarsity Press, 1980).

[9]Dante, *Paradiso* 33.145, trans. Mark Musa (New York: Penguin, 1980).

[10]Denise Levertov, "On Belief in the Physical Resurrection of Jesus," in *The Stream and the Sapphire* (New York: New Directions, 1997), 79-80.

[11]George Herbert, "Bitter Sweet," in *The English Poems of George Herbert*, ed. C. A. Patrides (London: Everyman, 1974), 176-77.

[12]Anya Silver, "Guest Post by Anya Silver: Motherhood and Mortality," *Dena Douglas Hobbs* (blog), May 19, 2015, https://denadouglashobbs.com/2015/05/guest-post-by-anya-silver-motherhood-and-mortality/.

9. OUR HOPE FOR YEARS TO COME

[1]Scott Carlson, "Caring Professor May Be Key in How a Graduate Thrives," *Chronicle of Higher Education*, May 6, 2014, www.chronicle.com/article/a-caring-professor-may-be-key-in-how-a-graduate-thrives/.

[2]Dante, *Inferno* 2.86-90, trans. Mark Musa (New York: Penguin, 1995).

[3]Dante, *Purgatorio* 15.67-75, trans. Mark Musa (New York: Penguin, 1995).

[4]Dante, *Paradiso* 3.64-75, 85, trans. Mark Musa (New York: Penguin, 1980).

[5]Rosemary Van Arsdel, "*Middlemarch* and the Modern American Student: Making the Cultural Leap," in *Approaches to Teaching Eliot's Middlemarch*, ed. Kathleen Blake (New York: MLA, 1990), 138.

[6]Pew Research Center, "Early Benchmarks Show 'Post-Millennials' On Track to Be Most Diverse, Best-Educated Generation Yet," November 13, 2018,

www.pewsocialtrends.org/2018/11/15/early-benchmarks-show-post-millennials
-on-track-to-be-most-diverse-best-educated-generation-yet/psdt-11-15-18_
postmillennials-00-01/.

[7]Pew Research Center, "Most U.S. Teens See Anxiety and Depression as a Major
Problem Among Their Peers," February 14, 2019, www.pewsocialtrends.org/2019
/02/20/most-u-s-teens-see-anxiety-and-depression-as-a-major-problem-among
-their-peers/psdt_02-20-19_teens-00-10/.

[8]Oyin Adedoyin, "As More Stressed-Out Students Consider Dropping Out,
Surgeon General Pushes College Leaders to Ramp Up Support," *Chronicle of
Higher Education* 69, no. 2. (August 2022).

[9]The Healthy Minds Study, Fall 2020 Data Report, https://healthymindsnetwork
.org/wp-content/uploads/2021/02/HMS-Fall-2020-National-Data-Report.pdf.

[10]Richard Wilbur, "The Writer," in *Collected Poems, 1943-2004* (Orlando: Harcourt,
2004), 128-29.

[11]George Eliot, *Scenes from Clerical Life*, ed. Thomas A. Noble (Oxford: Clarendon
Press, 1985), 256.

[12]Lionel Basney, "Dream of the School," in *Keeping Faith: Embracing the Tensions
in Christian Higher Education*, ed. Ronald A. Wells (Grand Rapids, MI: Eerdmans,
1996), 9.

Credits

Poetry

Images

Figure 1.1. *Agony in the Garden* by Fra Angelico, Santa Croce Monastery, Florence / photograph by Jennifer L. Holberg

Figure 1.2. *Pieter I Bruegel, The Fall of Icarus*, Royal Museums of Fine Arts of Belgium (Brussels), inv. 4030, photo: J. Geleyns

Figure 4.1. *The Deposition* by Michelangelo, Opera del Duomo Museum / photograph by Jennifer L. Holberg

Figure 5.1. The Plot Lines of Laurence Sterne's *Life and Opinions of Tristram Shandy, Gentleman*, drawn by the author, from the digitized first edition, 1767, Project Gutenberg / Wikimedia Commons

Figure 8.1. *Kintsugi Cup*, by Motoki Tonn / Unsplash / Free to use under the Unsplash License